wonders of Kansas!
Guidebook

Marci Penner

KANSAS SAMPLER FOUNDATION

Photographer **Harland J. Schuster**

Designer **Liz Penner King**

Editor **Bobbie Pray**

Introductory essays

Mil Penner

K. Vance Kelley

Jim Richardson

Josh Svaty

Dave Kendall

Martha Slater Farrell

Rex Buchanan

Leo E. Oliva

Julie Mulvihill

The Kansas Sampler Foundation's mission is to preserve and sustain rural culture by educating the public about what there is to see and do in Kansas and by networking and supporting rural communities. The Inman-based public non-profit is a 501(c)(3) organization.

The 8 Wonders of Kansas contest series was organized by the Kansas Sampler Foundation to inspire awareness of the beauty and value in Kansas, and to encourage travel. After the overall 8 Wonders of Kansas contest, the eight elements of rural culture were featured in their own contests. For more information about each entry, go to **www.8wonders.org.**

Mennonite Press, Inc., of Newton, our printer for this book and past publications, is a proud supporter of Kansas and the Kansas Sampler Foundation's efforts to help sustain Kansas communities and tell the Kansas story.

Printed in the United States of America by Mennonite Press, Inc., Newton, Kansas
Library of Congress Number 2011923042
ISBN: 978-0-9765408-1-6

Published by the Kansas Sampler Foundation
978 Arapaho Road, Inman, Kansas 67546
620.585.2374
marci@kansassampler.org, www.kansassampler.org

This book is dedicated to all Kansans

who take care of our resources and assets,

who are keepers and promoters of the story,

and who love to get out and explore

our great Sunflower State.

Makings of this book

By Marci Penner, Kansas Explorer #2, executive director of the Kansas Sampler Foundation

"Could you find someone to climb to the top of the water tower and pose with the red fish to show size perspective?"

"Do you think you could find about 80 kids and adults to stretch across main street at 7 p.m.?"

"Do you think you could find Buffalo Soldiers to pose?" *"Could you find someone on horseback to meet Harland at Castle Rock?"*

For this book, I made 216 photo arrangements for Harland Schuster, our photographer. As often as possible Harland wanted to take shots that weren't traditional. I kept shaking my head when he'd tell me what he wanted to do, but thanks to the tremendous cooperation from people across the state we pulled it off. The book you see today showcases these efforts.

The 8 Wonders of Kansas contest started in June 2007 and ended in October 2010. More than 100,000 people voted, including those from every state in the union and many foreign countries. The contest generated well over 1,000 articles, radio and TV stories, blogs, and Facebook mentions nationwide.

Unexpected results happened for those in the contest. Doniphan County graveled the road to 4-State Lookout when it became an 8 Wonder. Tony Prochaska at Trapper's in Simpson informed us he's been busier than ever since the contest started. Khan Nguyen from Pho Hoa said that his inclusion in the contest meant he was finally accepted into the community. Schermerhorn Park (Galena) folks reported that the contest made them feel a part of Kansas.

Families and groups used the 8 Wonders entries as destinations. Teachers applied the contest to class projects. Nursing home residents voted. Communities saw themselves with new eyes. Me? I fell deeper in love with Kansas. Writing summaries for the 216 places left me in awe of who we are and what we have in this state. My hope is that this book helps you know Kansas better and inspires you to explore every part it. Accept each place as it is: for its beauty, its entrepreneurial spirit, or for its effort to tell a story. The eight different "Wonder" categories, the contest, and this book provide a broad view of our state.

Sit back and enjoy 216 of the best places Kansas has to offer in Architecture, Art, Commerce, Cuisine, Customs, Geography, History, and People. Then, go! Visit as many as you can. If you do, you'll understand why Kansas is a state to love.

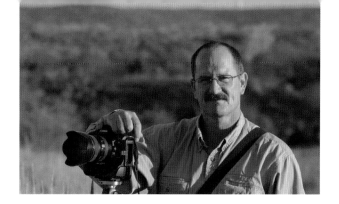

The photographic journey

By Harland J. Schuster, Kansas Explorer #1261, photographer and farmer

Kansas can be shy. She's not quick to flaunt her beauty at strangers. But for those who choose to slow down, to look deeper, she will reward their patience. My photographic efforts were aimed toward this goal—not to merely record the light reflected from the subjects, but to look deeper, to capture their essence, their soul. It was a photographic journey. One that carried me to the four corners of the Sunflower State, and to many equally intriguing places in between.

A photographer on assignment puts in some long days. Trading coffee for sleep just goes with the territory. On one fairly typical day I started by photographing a lake at sunrise, and then I was off for a few portraits of contented cows. Next, I found myself crawling out to the end of a fire truck ladder extended 25 feet over a swimming pool. An hour or so later I was racing to photograph ice cream before it melted at a soda fountain. Two hours following that, I was getting set for a panoramic shot at a small town where nearly all the inhabitants turned out to prove they had a big heart and a really wide main street. Lingering after sunset, I photographed the same street as the street lights flickered on one by one. And so it went. All along the way, I found myself receiving the gift of help from people who were not only willing to lend a hand to the effort but to go well beyond what would have been expected of them. To all these people, I express my sincere gratitude.

My thanks also go to Marci Penner, who had more faith in me than I had in myself, and proved this by offering me the privilege of doing the photography for this book. My deepest appreciation goes to my wife, Suzanne, whose support and encouragement made this work possible. And not to be forgotten are the photographers, art directors, and photo editors who have given me guidance through the years. In a very real way, it was their vision that guided me as I peered through the viewfinder.

Special thanks

First, to my sister, Liz King. Liz, your guidance and encouragement, your design expertise, your late hours, and the donation of your work make a book like this even possible. You did a beautiful job. From me, and on behalf of all Kansans, thank you— and thanks to your supportive family.

Harland Schuster, you win the photography endurance race! You had a lot of pictures to take in six months. I'm proud to feature your creative work in this book.

Bobbie Pray, thanks for another excellent editing job. Your knowledge of Kansas history was a bonus.

Thanks to all of you for the important roles you played: WenDee LaPlant, Mom and Dad, John and Debbie Divine, Ellen Morgan, Shelia Lampe, Gene Merry, Lynda Fort, Shari Wilson, Martha Slater Farrell, Steve Rudiger, Judy Entz, Suzanne Schuster, everyone who served on the contest selection committees, authors of the chapter introductions, and, especially, to all of the 8 Wonders of Kansas.

Von Rothenberger, thank you for coming to me with the idea to do the 7 Wonders of Kansas. We did 8, and look what happened!

The 8 Rural Culture Elements

In the early 1990s, as Dad (Mil Penner) and I researched our first guidebooks, we asked towns what they had that we could include. Too often the answer was that they didn't have anything. We decided to create categories (architecture, art, commerce, cuisine, customs, geography, history, and people) to help communities focus on who they are and what they have. Everything in a town fits into one of these categories, and every town has evidence or a story to tell about each category. The eight categories have become known as the Rural Culture Elements.

For more information about each entry, go to **www.8wonders.org.**

Contents

Overall **22**

Architecture **52**

Art **78**

Commerce **106**

Cuisine **132**

Customs **158**

Geography **188**

History **216**

People **242**

Sponsors **268**

Index **269**

Front cover: Gyp Hills. **p. 2:** Gyp Hills. **p. 4-15:** jam session, Cottonwood Falls; Haskell Indian Nations University, Lawrence; Konza Prairie, Manhattan; Holy Cross Church, Pfeifer; sun quilt, Red Barn Studio, Lindsborg; Tallgrass Prairie National Preserve, Strong City. **p. 16:** Gyp Hills. **p. 18:** round square, Blue Rapids. **p. 20-21:** Rock City, Minneapolis. **p. 21:** Mahaffie Stagecoach Stop and Farm Historic Site, Olathe.

Overall Top 8 Wonders

Big Well, Greensburg

Castle Rock and Monument Rocks, Gove County

Cheyenne Bottoms and Quivira National Wildlife Refuge, Barton and Stafford Counties

Dwight D. Eisenhower Presidential Library and Museum, Abilene

Kansas Cosmosphere and Space Center, Hutchinson

Kansas Underground Salt Museum, Hutchinson

St. Fidelis Church (Cathedral of the Plains), Victoria

Tallgrass Prairie National Preserve (Flint Hills), Chase County

Overall Finalist Wonders

Arikaree Breaks, Cheyenne County

Ball of Twine, Cawker City

Big Brutus, West Mineral

Blackbear Bosin's *Keeper of the Plains*, Wichita

Brookville Hotel, Abilene

Chase County Courthouse, Cottonwood Falls

Cimarron National Grassland, Morton County

Constitution Hall State Historic Site, Lecompton

Davis Memorial, Hiawatha

Fort Larned National Historic Site, Larned

Garden of Eden, Lucas

Gypsum Hills Scenic Drive, Barber County

John Steuart Curry Murals, Topeka

Lake Scott State Park, Scott County

Pawnee Indian Museum State Historic Site, Republic County

St. Mary's Catholic Church, St. Benedict

The Wonders of Kansas

By Mil Penner, farmer, contractor, photographer, and author

Rising from desert sands in Egypt, the immense pyramid of Cheops still inspires awe and wonder as the last remaining Seven Wonders of the World. We tend to feel that its colossal size, its antiquity, and its ethereal appeal have been unchallenged throughout the ages.

Yet, as I traveled Kansas, photographing and exploring, countless new wonders appeared if I would look with new eyes attuned to see the commonplace in depth. The challenge of immensity was easily met by observing the expanding panorama of a Flint Hills sunrise or the dimensions of outer space as featured in Hutchinson's Kansas Cosmosphere and Space Center.

Antiquity presented no contest. Preserved in remnants of chalk beds at Castle Rock and Monument Rocks are fossilized skeletons of fish and reptiles that sank to the bottom of an inland sea eons ago.

Rivaling the pyramid tribute to King Cheops, Abilene's Dwight Eisenhower Presidential Library and Museum is a tribute to a great warrior, statesman, and builder of a nation's road complex greater than all of Egypt.

Above all, the wonders of Kansas touch the soul. Wandering roads beyond worldly cares display vibrant wildflowers as sandpipers trill melodiously from fence posts. I love the land of Kansas.

THE BIG WELL, Greensburg

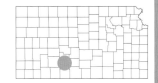

TOP 8 WONDER: *The Big Well is one of the 8 Wonders of Kansas because its construction was an engineering marvel in its day (1887), and it is the world's largest hand-dug well.*

On August 9, 1887, Jack Wheeler led his crew in an architectural adventure as the first shovel dug into what would become a 32-foot-wide, 109-foot-deep well with two-foot-thick native stone walls. Taking a year to complete, the well was hand dug, cribbed, and cased and stoned with rock from the Medicine River and sand from Cowskin Creek.

Although the well was built to supply water to the town of Greensburg, it was also constructed alongside the Kingman, Pratt, & Western rail line to supply water for steam locomotives. The Big Well supplied Greensburg with water until 1932 when another well was dug nearby.

In 1939 the folks of Greensburg decided to place a handmade sign along the highway and begin promoting their well as a Kansas tourism site.

On May 4, 2007, Greensburg was hit by the monster EF5 tornado that destroyed much of the town, including everything above ground at the Big Well. Currently the Big Well is not open for visitation, but plans are to build a museum on the site and open it once again to the public sometime in 2012.

LOCATION
315 S. Sycamore,
Greensburg 67054

CONTACTS
620.723.4102;
info@bigwell.org;
www.bigwell.org

explorer extras...

Rebuilding Greensburg since the tornado has been an impressive achievement, and the town's commitment to rebuild "green" is evident in the 5.4.7 Arts Center, 204 W. Wisconsin; www.547artscenter.org; Monday, Wednesday, Friday 2-6 p.m.; Tuesday, Thursday 9 a.m.-12 p.m. Learn more about the town's remarkable recovery efforts at the "Green" Visitor Center and the Silo Eco-Home, 402 S. Sycamore, Greensburg; 620.723.2790; www.greensburggreentown.org.
ee

CASTLE ROCK AND MONUMENT ROCKS, Gove County

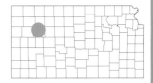

TOP 8 WONDER: *Castle Rock and Monument Rocks are one of the 8 Wonders of Kansas because of the scientifically significant fossils these ancient chalk beds have produced, and because they have been highly eroded into unusual spires and shapes, making them spectacular landmarks on the plains of western Kansas.*

LOCATION
From I-70 Quinter exit 107 (Castle Rock Road), 15 miles south to the intersection of GO 80 and GO K, 4 miles east to Castle Rock sign, and north across a cattle guard (dry weather road only).

CONTACTS
785.754.3538; quintertreas@ruraltel.net; www.naturalkansas.org/castle.htm

On the western edge of Gove County, Monument Rocks comprises a series of large, heavily sculpted chalk monoliths that are sometimes referred to as the Chalk Pyramids. The site has been designated as a National Natural Landmark. Castle Rock, in eastern Gove County, is a chalk spire standing alone in a cattle pasture. Both formations continue to change shape because the chalk is easily eroded. The tallest spire at Castle Rock fell following a 2001 thunderstorm. The configuration of Monument Rocks famous keyhole arch alters slightly each year.

The chalk was deposited during the Cretaceous period, about 80 million years ago, when the central interior of the United States was covered by a seaway. The ocean, which was several hundred feet deep, contained single-celled animals that drifted to the sea floor for eons, creating a mucky ooze. This material was perfect for trapping and preserving the remains of animals that lived in that ocean, such as fish, turtles, sharks, swimming reptiles called mosasaurs and plesiosaurs, swimming birds, and gliding reptiles called pterosaurs, as well as invertebrate animals. Probably the best known fossil from these beds is the famous "fish-within-a-fish" on display at the Sternberg Museum in Hays.

Both Monument Rocks and Castle Rock are on private property, but the landowners are amenable to visitors and no special permission is required. Please be respectful.

explorer extras...

Continue southward about a half mile on the rutted road from Castle Rock to the "badlands." More intriguing in many ways than the iconic Castle Rock is this playground of chalk residue and interesting formations. Two dozen Castle Rock photographs dating to 1894 adorn the Pizza Station, 1300 Castle Rock Road, south side of I-70 at #107 exit, Quinter; 785.754.2400; Monday-Friday 11 a.m.-2 p.m. and 5-9 p.m.; Saturday-Sunday 5-9 p.m. **ee**

MONUMENT ROCKS

LOCATION
20 miles south of
Oakley on U.S. 83,
4 miles east on Jayhawk
Road; 3 miles south,
and 1 mile east
(dry weather road only);
or 18 miles north of
Scott City on U.S. 83,
2 miles east on Dakota
Road, 1 mile north,
3½ miles east,
and 2½ miles north.

CONTACTS
620.872.2762; keystone@
keystonegallery.com;
www.keystonegallery.com/
area/monument_rocks.html

explorer extras...
*Visit Chuck Bonner
and Barbara Shelton's
fossil museum and
art gallery, located
in a 1917 church,
to learn about fossils
and the fascinating
history of the area
chalk beds. Keystone
Gallery, 401 U.S. 83,
Scott City; 26 miles
south of Oakley,
or 18 miles north
of Scott City;
620.872.2762.* **ee**

CHEYENNE BOTTOMS AND QUIVIRA NATIONAL WILDLIFE REFUGE, Barton and Stafford Counties

TOP 8 WONDER: *The Kansas wetlands complex comprising Cheyenne Bottoms and Quivira National Wildlife Refuge is one of the 8 Wonders of Kansas because of its vital and international importance as a migratory stop for North American shorebirds.*

LOCATION
6 miles north of Great Bend on U.S. 281, then 2 miles east; or 5 miles south of Hoisington on U.S. 281, then 2 miles east.

CONTACTS
620.793.3066; cheybott@ksoutdoors.com; www.kdwp.state.ks.us

HOURS
Always open.

CHEYENNE BOTTOMS

Cheyenne Bottoms is a 41,000-acre lowland basin and is the largest fresh-water marsh in the interior of the United States. It is considered the most important shorebird migration point in the Western Hemisphere. Each year this area attracts approximately 45 percent of all shorebirds moving through North America during spring migration and 90 percent of a few species such as long-billed dowitchers, Baird's sandpipers, and a few others. At least 320 species of birds have been recorded. The area is a critical habitat for several threatened and endangered species such as whooping cranes, Peregrine falcons, least terns, and piping plovers. Thousands of sandhill cranes stop here on their spring and fall migrations. Visitors can drive or walk along the dikes for some magnificent bird watching.

explorer extras...

Drive the Wetlands and Wildlife National Scenic Byway, which curves around Cheyenne Bottoms and Quivira National Wildlife Refuge for 76 miles. A good beginning point is K-4 and U.S. 281 near Hoisington. Learn more at the Kansas Wetlands Education Center, 592 NE U.S. 156, Great Bend; 10 miles northeast of U.S. 281 and U.S. 56/156; 877.243.9268; http://wetlandscenter.fhsu.edu; Tuesday-Saturday 8 a.m.-5 p.m.; Sunday 1-5 p.m. **ee**

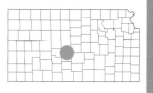

LOCATION
7 miles north of
U.S. 50 (at Stafford)
to a four-way stop, then
6 miles east to the
Quivira Refuge sign,
and 1 mile north.

CONTACTS
620.486.2393;
quivira@fws.gov;
www.fws.gov/quivira

HOURS
Always open.

QUIVIRA NATIONAL WILDLIFE REFUGE

Less than 20 miles from Cheyenne Bottoms,
Quivira National Wildlife Refuge is 22,135 acres of
sand prairie, saltwater marsh, and other wetlands.
During spring migration it is a staging area for more
than 500,000 birds. Big and Little Salt Marshes are
ancient basins that attract thousands of migratory
waterfowl, providing them with food, cover, and
a place to rest during exhausting flights between
breeding and wintering areas.

explorer extras...

*The Quivira National Wildlife Refuge Visitor
Center, at the south end of the refuge, offers
animal pelts to touch, bird songs to hear,
and fascinating migratory bird information
including locations of the birds. 1434 NE 80th,
Stafford; 620.486.2393; www.fws.gov/quivira;
Monday-Friday 7:30 a.m.-4 p.m.*

DWIGHT D. EISENHOWER PRESIDENTIAL LIBRARY AND MUSEUM, Abilene

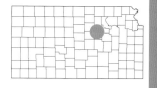

TOP 8 WONDER: *The Eisenhower Presidential Library and Museum is one of the 8 Wonders of Kansas because it tells of the remarkable lifetime achievements of Dwight D. Eisenhower, five-star general and U.S. president.*

Dwight D. Eisenhower commanded the largest amphibious military operation in history: the 1944 Allied invasion of Nazi controlled Western Europe. His many military achievements are interpreted superbly in the galleries at the Eisenhower Museum.

Eisenhower is the only five-star general to become a U.S. president. The exhibits interpret the highlights of his two terms (1953-1961) in office. Significantly, his administration initiated the nation's first civil rights legislation since 1875. More than any other president, Eisenhower was responsible for the Interstate Highway System. He also became known as the first "television president."

Five galleries at the museum tell Eisenhower's story, from his childhood days in Abilene through his retirement years. One gallery represents the life and lifestyle of one of America's most beloved first ladies, Mamie Eisenhower.

Visitors can also tour the 19th-century frame house, on its original site, where the Eisenhower family lived from 1898 until the death of the president's mother, Ida, in 1946. The Presidential Library is a major research facility containing millions of manuscripts, photographs, and much more. The Place of Meditation is the final resting place of the president, his wife, and their first-born son, Doud Dwight. A larger-than-life statue of General Eisenhower is at the center of the campus.

explorer extras...

Mr. K's Farmhouse restaurant, formerly known as Lena's, was frequented by President Eisenhower. Lena used to paddle guests on their birthdays, and even Eisenhower wasn't immune on his 75th. See the paddle Mamie Eisenhower signed and ask to sit in chairs that Ike and Mamie used. 407 S. Van Buren, Abilene; 3rd to Van Buren, then 2 miles south on Old U.S. 40; 785.263.7995; www.mrksfarmhouse.com; Tuesday-Saturday 11 a.m.-2 p.m. and 5-9 p.m.; Sunday 11 a.m.-2 p.m. **ee**

LOCATION
200 SE 4th,
Abilene 67410

CONTACTS
785.263.6700;
eisenhower.library@
nara.gov;
www.eisenhower.
archives.gov

HOURS
Memorial Day to
mid-August
daily 8 a.m.-5:45 p.m.;
mid-August to
Memorial Day daily
9 a.m.-4:45 p.m.;
closed major holidays.
Admission charge.

KANSAS COSMOSPHERE AND SPACE CENTER, Hutchinson

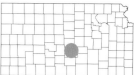

TOP 8 WONDER: *The Kansas Cosmosphere and Space Center is one of the 8 Wonders of Kansas because it has one of the most significant collections of U.S. and Russian space artifacts in the world.*

The Kansas Cosmosphere and Space Center, conceived by longtime Hutchinson resident Patricia Carey, is one of America's premier space centers. Making its start as a small planetarium on the Kansas State Fairgrounds, the Cosmosphere is now an internationally acclaimed staple of the space science community.

Educating patrons from around the globe, the Cosmosphere boasts the Hall of Space Museum, containing U.S. and Russian space artifacts; the Carey IMAX Dome Theater®, one of only 14 IMAX® dome theaters in the world; a planetarium; and space-themed training camps for all ages.

The Cosmosphere's Hall of Space Museum is one of only three museums in the world to exhibit flown spacecraft from all three early-manned space programs: Mercury (Liberty Bell 7), Gemini (Gemini 10), and Apollo (Apollo 13).

With regard to depth and size, the Cosmosphere's space artifact collection is second only to that of the National Air and Space Museum in Washington, D.C. Similarly, the Cosmosphere's Hall of Space Museum harbors the largest collection of Russian space artifacts outside Moscow.

explorer extras...

Although captivating artifacts fill the Hall of Space Museum, the human element creates the drama. The gripping story of the people—from the German scientist defectors to astronauts and cosmonauts—who influenced the space evolution is told through tapes and video. **ee**

LOCATION
1100 N. Plum,
Hutchinson 67501

CONTACTS
800.397.0330;
info@cosmo.org;
www.cosmo.org

HOURS
Monday-Thursday
9 a.m.-5 p.m.; Friday-
Saturday 9 a.m.-7 p.m.;
Sunday 12-5 p.m.;
check Web site for
schedule changes and
IMAX show times.
Admission charge.

KANSAS UNDERGROUND SALT MUSEUM, Hutchinson

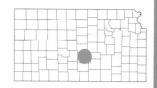

TOP 8 WONDER: *The Kansas Underground Salt Museum is one of the 8 Wonders of Kansas because it showcases a natural treasure, salt, hundreds of feet below the Kansas plains.*

Hutchinson seized the unique opportunity to provide a destination attraction for visitors to explore an exotic environ carved from salt deposits formed 275 million years ago, 650 feet below the surface.

The United States contains 16 salt mines, but Hutchinson has the only one, in fact the only one in the Western Hemisphere, with an underground museum open to tourists. Only two other underground salt museums exist in the world; one in Poland and the other in Austria.

The adventure at the Kansas Underground Salt Museum begins on board a double-decked elevator that takes visitors to the salt deposit 650 feet down. Upon arriving underground, visitors may wander through exhibits that tell the story of salt mining, the geologic history of the area, and how these vast salt caverns under Hutchinson have been used to store millions of items in a separate secure area. Visitors have the option of boarding a tram that takes them into mined-out areas or taking a train that rolls over rails and ties originally used to haul salt. From the train, visitors will see naturally occurring geologic formations and artifacts that miners left behind during an 85-year period.

LOCATION
3504 E. Avenue G, Hutchinson 67501. Avenue G and Airport Road, 1 mile north of U.S. 50 and Yoder Road.

CONTACTS
620.662.1425; info@underground museum.org; www.underground museum.org

HOURS
Summer, Tuesday-Saturday 9 a.m.-6 p.m.; Sunday 1-6 p.m. Winter, Tuesday-Friday 9 a.m.-5 p.m.; Saturday 9 a.m.-6 p.m.; Sunday 1-6 p.m.; last tour daily is 2 hours prior to closing; check Web site for holiday hours. Reservations recommended. Admission charge.

explorer extras...

See actual movie costumes and props, from the underground vaults storage, exhibited at the Salt Museum. They include the cricket gun and sunglasses from Men in Black, *George Clooney's Batman costume, and Arnold Swartzenegger's Mr. Freeze outfit from* Batman & Robin. **ee**

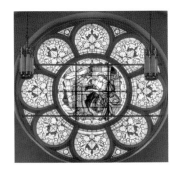

ST. FIDELIS CHURCH, Victoria

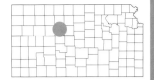

TOP 8 WONDER: *St. Fidelis Church is one of the 8 Wonders of Kansas because of the architectural grandeur and the impressive craftsmanship achieved by the area's Volga German pioneers.*

If you are anywhere near Victoria, you can't miss the twin bell towers of St. Fidelis rising majestically above the plains. With a seating capacity of 1,100, St. Fidelis was the largest church west of the Mississippi when it was completed in 1911. Its beauty and size inspired William Jennings Bryan (visiting the area in 1912 on a presidential campaign tour) to dub it the "Cathedral of the Plains."

The stone for this massive Romanesque structure came from a quarry seven miles south of the church. Extracting the stone, loading it, hauling it, and then dressing it was a gigantic task and an amazing feat accomplished without automatic lifts and power tools.

The church structure is a cruciform (built in the shape of a cross), 220 feet long and 110 feet wide at the transepts and 75 feet wide at the nave. The massive twin bell towers are 141 feet tall. The granite pillars were shipped from Vermont.

Native son Wayne Brungardt was the architect of the 1990s St. Fidelis restoration. Tim Linenberger repainted and intricately re-stenciled the interior, returning it to its original rich mauve and gold tones.

explorer extras...

Across the street from St. Fidelis, Pete Felten stone sculptures depict a Volga German family. The statues memorialize the hardworking colonists from Saratov, Russia, who immigrated to Victoria in 1876. **ee**

LOCATION
601 10th,
Victoria 67671

CONTACTS
785.735.2777;
fidelis@ruraltel.net;
www.stfidelischurch.com

HOURS
Open daily.

TALLGRASS PRAIRIE NATIONAL PRESERVE, Chase County

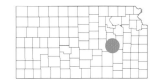

TOP 8 WONDER: *The Tallgrass Prairie National Preserve is one of the 8 Wonders of Kansas because it represents the last significant example of the tallgrass prairie in North America.*

Tallgrass prairie once covered approximately 170 million acres of North America. It was the continent's largest continuous ecosystem. Its grasses include big bluestem, little bluestem, Indian grass, and switchgrass, all of which can grow to heights of eight feet by summer's end, depending on moisture and other factors.

Because prairie soils produce outstanding crops, man has plowed the prairie everywhere possible for domestic crop production. Today less than 4 percent of the prairie remains, most of it in the Kansas Flint Hills, making it one of the rarest and most endangered ecosystems in the world.

In 1996, to protect this vanishing landscape, Congress created the 10,894-acre Tallgrass National Prairie Preserve in the Flint Hills north of Strong City. The National Park Service restored the 1881 Spring Hill Farm and Stock Ranch, located on the preserve, to help tell the area's cultural story. In the spring of 2010, 13 bison were added to the preserve.

Prairie bus tours into the preserve are offered seasonally, and hiking trails are open 24 hours a day, year-round. Self-guided tours of the beautiful Spring Hill Farm and Stock Ranch also are available.

LOCATION
2480 K-177,
Strong City 66869.
2 miles north of
Strong City on K-177;
or 17 miles south
of Council Grove
on K-177.

CONTACTS
620.273.8494;
www.nps.gov/tapr

HOURS
Spring Hill Ranch open
daily 9 a.m.-4:30 p.m.;
closed major holidays.

explorer extras...
To see the panoramic vistas of the tallgrass prairie, drive the 47 miles of the Flint Hills National Scenic Byway on K-177 between Council Grove and Cassoday. 800.684.6966; www.ksbyways.org. **ee**

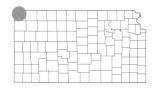

ARIKAREE BREAKS, Cheyenne County

8 WONDER FINALIST: *Arikaree Breaks is a finalist for the 8 Wonders of Kansas because its deep and rugged canyons create a distinct and scenically dramatic Kansas landscape.*

LOCATION
Go north from the Benton and Washington intersection in St. Francis, cross the Republican River bridge, and turn right at the first fork. Watch for the numbered red-disk signs as you go north into Nebraska on Road 15 (unpaved). In Nebraska, go west on U.S. 34 to Haigler and turn south to K-27. A self-guided driving tour brochure is available at the Cheyenne County Museum and online at stfranciskansas.com, click on Area Attractions.

CONTACTS
785.332.3142;
clerk@cityofstfrancis.net

For more information, see page 208.

The Breaks were formed during the past few million years from windblown silt called loess. As water eroded loess deposits, steep-sided canyons formed. Surrounded by plains, the Arikaree Breaks, in the most northwestern county of the state, is covered by short-grass prairie, particularly buffalo grass, yucca plants, and prickly pear cactus.

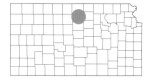

BALL OF TWINE, Cawker City

8 WONDER FINALIST: *The Ball of Twine is a finalist for the 8 Wonders of Kansas because it is a legendary Kansas icon and the world's largest ball of sisal twine that is still expanding.*

LOCATION
Downtown Cawker City; south side of U.S. 24.

CONTACTS
785.781.4470;
clover@nckcn.com

For more information, see page 186.

Frank Stoeber started winding twine on his farm on December 24, 1953. In 1961 his "symbol of thrift" had grown so large it was moved to Cawker City so all could see it. Visitors continue to add to the Ball of Twine, and as of January 1, 2011, it weighed 19,716 pounds and was 8,028,100 feet (or 1,520.47 miles) long!

BIG BRUTUS, West Mineral

8 WONDER FINALIST: *Big Brutus is a finalist for the 8 Wonders of Kansas because it is the largest electric coal shovel in the world, and as a museum, it represents the coal mining industry of southeast Kansas.*

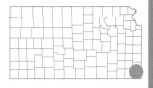

Designed and built by Bucyrus-Erie, the 1850-B coal shovel is the only one of its kind ever built.

It ran 24 hours a day, seven days a week from 1963 until 1974 and moved approximately one square mile each year. The huge bucket removed the overburden before huge coal strippers moved in on the coal seams.

LOCATION
6509 NW 60th,
West Mineral 66782.
7 miles north of
Columbus on K-7,
6 miles west on K-102,
and ½ mile south.

CONTACTS
620.827.6177;
bigbrutus@
columbus-ks.com;
www.bigbrutus.org

HOURS
January to March
daily 10 a.m.-4 p.m.;
April through May
daily 9 a.m.-5 p.m.;
Memorial Day to Labor
Day daily 9 a.m.-7 p.m.;
Labor Day to January
daily 9 a.m.-5 p.m.
Admission charge.

For more information, see page 109.

BLACKBEAR BOSIN'S *KEEPER OF THE PLAINS,* Wichita

8 WONDER FINALIST: Keeper of the Plains *is a finalist for the 8 Wonders of Kansas because it is an awe-inspiring sculpture by well-known artist Blackbear Bosin that honors the region's original citizens and has become a symbol of Wichita.*

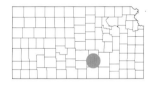

The majestic 44-foot, five-ton *Keeper of the Plains* was designed by Blackbear Bosin (1921-1980), a Kiowa-Comanche and internationally recognized artist, muralist, and designer. The colossal steel statue was placed at the confluence of the Little Arkansas and Arkansas Rivers, which is considered a sacred site by some Native Americans and was home to the Wichita tribe for many years.

LOCATION
650 N. Seneca,
Wichita 67203

CONTACTS
316.350.3340;
www.wichita.gov/City
Offices/Culture/Keeper

HOURS
Daily 5 a.m.-midnight

For more information, see page 83.

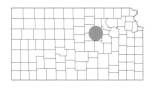

BROOKVILLE HOTEL, Abilene

8 WONDER FINALIST: *Brookville Hotel is a finalist for the 8 Wonders of Kansas because of its famous family-style chicken dinners that have been pleasing crowds since 1915. Originally located in the small town of Brookville, the restaurant was inside the town's historic hotel.*

LOCATION
105 E. Lafayette Avenue, Abilene 67410

CONTACTS
785.263.2244; cdmartin@ brookvillehotel.com; www.brookvillehotel.com

HOURS
Wednesday-Friday 5-7:30 p.m.; Saturday 11:30 a.m.-2 p.m. and 4:30-7:30 p.m.; Sunday 11:30 a.m.-2 p.m. and 5-7 p.m. Reservations recommended.

For more information, see page 137.

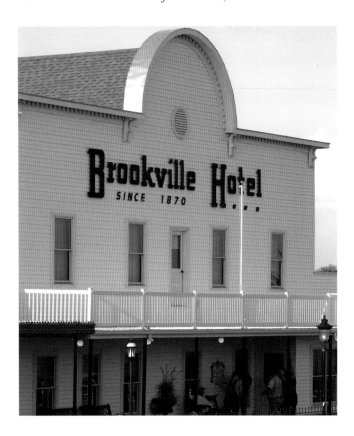

Relishes, sweet-sour slaw, skillet-fried chicken, mashed potatoes and cream gravy, cream-style corn, baking powder biscuits with creamy butter and preserves, and home-style ice cream—that's the famous Brookville Hotel menu.

CHASE COUNTY COURTHOUSE, Cottonwood Falls

8 WONDER FINALIST: *Chase County Courthouse is a finalist for the 8 Wonders of Kansas because of its striking French Renaissance (Second Empire) style and red mansard roof, which make it one of the most recognizable buildings in Kansas.*

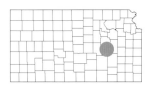

LOCATION
308 Broadway, Cottonwood Falls 66845

CONTACTS
620.273.8469; chasechamber@ sbcglobal.net

HOURS
Monday-Friday 8 a.m.-5 p.m.

For more information, see page 55.

Designed by noted Kansas architect John G. Haskell and completed in 1873, it is the oldest county courthouse in use in Kansas.

The French Renaissance (Second Empire) style is characterized by the roof's distinctive shape. Standing 113 feet tall, the courthouse and its red mansard roof are visible from vantage points throughout the county.

CIMARRON NATIONAL GRASSLAND, Morton County

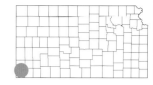

8 WONDER FINALIST: *Cimarron National Grassland is a finalist for the 8 Wonders of Kansas because of its early pioneering advancements in conservation, it contains the longest publicly owned section of the historic Santa Fe Trail, and it features three ecosystems (shortgrass prairie, sand-sage prairie, and wooded riparian).*

After the devastating dust storms of the 1930s, the federal government bought land to take out of production and thereby help control wind erosion.

The largest tract of public land in Kansas, this area was designated a national grassland in 1954. The 108,000 acres offer an abundance of prairie flowers, wildlife, and birding opportunities.

LOCATION
2 miles north of Elkhart on K-27 in Morton County.

CONTACTS
620.697.4621;
sharilbutler@fs.fed.us;
www.fs.usda.gov/goto/psicc/cim

For more information, see page 210.

CONSTITUTION HALL STATE HISTORIC SITE, Lecompton

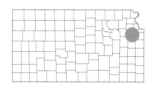

8 WONDER FINALIST: *Constitution Hall State Historic Site is a finalist for the 8 Wonders of Kansas because the events that transpired inside this two-story, frame building were highly significant in igniting the Civil War.*

LOCATION
319 Elmore,
Lecompton 66050

CONTACTS
785.887.6520;
consthall@kshs.org;
www.kshs.org/portal_constitution_hall

HOURS
Wednesday-Saturday
9 a.m.-5 p.m.;
Sunday 1-5 p.m.
Admission charge.

For more information, see page 235.

The proslavery Lecompton Constitution, drafted here in 1857, was a major event leading to the war. The North was determined to stop the expansion of slavery into Kansas, and the South was equally determined that Kansas would become a slave state. In 1858 President James Buchanan urged Congress to admit Kansas to the Union as a slave state under the Lecompton Constitution, but the constitution was rejected.

DAVIS MEMORIAL, Hiawatha

8 WONDER FINALIST: *The Davis Memorial is a finalist for the 8 Wonders of Kansas because of its grandeur, and because of the controversy that surrounded this massive cemetery memorial.*

LOCATION
Mount Hope Cemetery, ½ mile east on Iowa from U.S. 73 in Hiawatha.

CONTACTS
785.742.7136; hiawathachamber@ rainbowtel.net; www.kansastravel.org/ davismemorial.htm

For more information, see page 99.

John Davis and his wife, Sarah, moved to Hiawatha in 1915 and lived ordinary lives. When Sarah died in 1930, John erected an imposing marble memorial to her in Mount Hope Cemetery. Soon 11 Italian marble or granite life-sized statues were positioned around it. The community was intensely critical and suspected that Davis' extravagance was intended more as a slap in the face to his wife's heirs than as a tribute to Sarah.

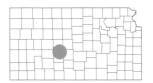

FORT LARNED NATIONAL HISTORIC SITE, Larned

8 WONDER FINALIST: *Fort Larned National Historic Site is a finalist for the 8 Wonders of Kansas because it is one of the best preserved authentic frontier posts in the American West.*

LOCATION
6 miles west of Larned on K-156.

CONTACTS
620.285.6911; fols_internet@nps.gov; www.nps.gov/fols

HOURS
Daily 8:30 a.m.-5 p.m.

For more information, see page 237.

Established in 1859 to protect the U.S. mail and Santa Fe Trail traffic, the fort also kept peace on the plains during the Civil War and the Plains Indian wars. After the construction of its native-stone buildings in 1867-1868, Fort Larned was a premier post.

The National Park Service acquired the site in 1964. Today the fort comprises nine original stone structures (including the post hospital, bakery, blacksmith shop, enlisted men's barracks, mess hall, officers' quarters, and storehouses) and a reconstructed blockhouse.

GARDEN OF EDEN, Lucas

8 WONDER FINALIST: *The Garden of Eden is a finalist for the 8 Wonders of Kansas because it is one of the top ten contemporary folk art sites in the world.*

In 1905, at the age of 64, Civil War veteran Samuel Perry Dinsmoor began constructing this unusual site by building his home of limestone logs. Then, using 113 tons of cement, Dinsmoor built more than a dozen concrete trees to hold his 50 larger-than-life figures in his sculpture garden, which interprets his views of Populist politics, modern civilization, and the Bible.

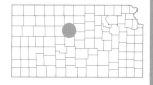

LOCATION
Kansas and 2nd,
Lucas 67648

CONTACTS
785.525.6395;
lucascoc@wtciweb.com;
www.garden-of-eden-lucas-kansas.com

HOURS
May through October daily 10 a.m.-5 p.m.; November through February, Saturday-Sunday 1-4 p.m.; March through April daily 1-4 p.m. Admission charge.

For more information, see pages 88, 89.

GYP HILLS SCENIC DRIVE, Barber County

8 WONDER FINALIST: *Gyp Hills Scenic Drive is a finalist for the 8 Wonders of Kansas because it showcases the stunning rust-red buttes and mesas capped by layers of sparkling white gypsum.*

LOCATION
Approximately 4 miles west of Medicine Lodge on U.S. 160. At the sign reading "Gyp Hills Scenic Drive," go south on Gypsum Hill Road, then west. Watch for and follow the small green signs. Much of the route is unpaved. At about 22 miles, the route comes back north to U.S. 160 at the Lake City Road. The Gyp Hills Scenic Drive and the Gypsum Hills Scenic Byway (along U.S. 160 between Medicine Lodge and Coldwater) are two different routes.

CONTACTS
620.886.3553;
earlkuhn@sbcglobal.net

For more information, see page 197.

Many rocks and much of the soil are stained red by iron oxide, thus giving the name Red Hills to the area. Sandstone and shale, in particular, are bright red. Gypsum, a white rock, is found in layers within those red beds.

Much of this 22-mile route is through open range. Wildlife, native grasses, wildflowers, birds, and cattle dominate the landscape against the Red Hills.

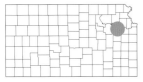

JOHN STEUART CURRY MURALS, Topeka

8 WONDER FINALIST: *The John Steuart Curry murals are a finalist for the 8 Wonders of Kansas because Curry was one of the greatest American Regionalist artists, and because he considered the state capitol murals his greatest work.*

In June 1937 John Steuart Curry was commissioned to paint murals in the Kansas statehouse. However, before he could finish, his work was criticized. As a result, Curry refused to sign and complete all that he had planned. *Tragic Prelude*, the most famous of his finished murals, is the artist's interpretation of John Brown and the antislavery movement in Kansas Territory.

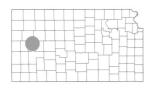

LOCATION
Kansas State Capitol,
300 SW 10th,
Topeka 66612

CONTACTS
785.296.3966;
capitol@kshs.org;
www.kshs.org/
portal_capitol

HOURS
Monday-Friday
8 a.m.-5 p.m.; guided
tours available at the
Capitol Visitor Center.

For more information,
see page 95.

LAKE SCOTT STATE PARK, Scott County

8 WONDER FINALIST: *Lake Scott State Park is a finalist for the 8 Wonders of Kansas because of its history, its role as an oasis in an otherwise dry land, and its craggy canyons, which provide a sudden and surprising landscape on the High Plains of western Kansas.*

Lake Scott rests in a valley carved into the steep bluffs of the Ogallala formation. Composed of naturally cemented sand and gravels, the rocks rim the steep canyons and draws that surround the 100-acre spring-fed natural lake. Famous sites within the park are El Cuartelejo (ruins of a late-1600s Indian pueblo) and the 1909 Steele Homestead.

LOCATION
101 W. Scott Lake Drive,
Scott City 67871.
10 miles north of
Scott City on U.S. 83,
then 3 miles northwest
on K-95.

CONTACTS
620.872.2061;
scottsp@ksoutdoors.com;
www.kdwp.state.ks.us

HOURS
Daily 24 hours. State
park entrance charge.

For more information,
see page 212.

PAWNEE INDIAN MUSEUM STATE HISTORIC SITE, Republic

8 WONDER FINALIST: *Pawnee Indian Museum State Historic Site is a finalist for the 8 Wonders of Kansas because it is one of the only museums in the Central Plains that tells the story and preserves the remains of an early indigenous tribe.*

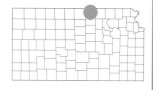

During the 1700s approximately 1,500 Pawnee Indians resided on this site in their earth-lodge village. In winter and summer they temporarily left the area to follow the buffalo herds.

In 1967 a museum was built over one large excavated lodge floor. Still visible are ashes in the fireplace, post holes, bone hoes, burned corn, trade hoes, and tool-making equipment.

LOCATION
480 Pawnee Trail, Republic 66964. 8 miles north of U.S. 36 on K-266 in Republic County.

CONTACTS
785.361.2255;
piv@kshs.org;
www.kshs.org/portal_pawnee_indian

HOURS
Wednesday-Saturday 9 a.m.-5 p.m.; Sunday 1-5 p.m. Admission charge.

For more information, see page 241.

ST. MARY'S CATHOLIC CHURCH, St. Benedict

8 WONDER FINALIST: *St. Mary's Catholic Church is a finalist for the 8 Wonders of Kansas because of the grandeur of its lavish ornamentation, leaded windows, statuary, and murals. Additionally, it is the only known well-preserved church whose interior decor is by artist G.F. Satory.*

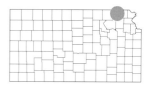

In 1901 Satory decorated St. Mary's with symbolic art by painting beautifully colored patterns, bands, and friezes on the walls, ceiling, cast iron columns, vault ribs, and window openings.

Adding to the interior's rich decor are 14 large oil paintings by Russian-born artist Th. Zukotynski, six Bavarian-made transept windows, and eight lead-glazed side windows.

LOCATION
1 mile west of Seneca on U.S. 36, 3 miles north on K-178, then ½ mile west.

CONTACTS
office@stmstb.org;
www.stmstb.org

HOURS
Daily 8 a.m.-5 p.m.

For more information, see page 97.

Overall

Architecture Top 8 Wonders

Chase County Courthouse, Cottonwood Falls

Cooper Barn, Colby

Fromme-Birney Round Barn, Mullinville

Holy Cross Church, Pfeifer

Kansas State Capitol, Topeka

Lebold Mansion, Abilene

Ness County Bank, Ness City

Seelye Mansion, Abilene

Architecture Finalist Wonders

Adobe House (formerly known as Peter Paul Loewen House), Hillsboro

Brown Mansion, Coffeyville

Chapel of the Veterans, Leavenworth

Dyche Hall, Lawrence

Franklin County Courthouse, Ottawa

Historic Fox Theatre, Hutchinson

John Mack Bridge, Wichita

Mary Queen of Peace Catholic Church, Ulysses

Masonic Center, Salina

Muchnic Home and Gallery, Atchison

Osborne County Courthouse, Osborne

St. Joseph Church, Damar

Samson of the Cimarron, Seward County

Topeka High School, Topeka

Wichita Carthalite, Wichita

Windsor Hotel, Garden City

K. Vance Kelley, historic preservation architect

As an architect in the field of historic preservation, I'm often asked, "Are there any buildings in Kansas worth preserving?" My answer is clear and simple. Kansas has a vast treasure-trove of architecture that is significant and unique!

Our architectural treasures range from vernacular agricultural buildings to the monumental churches and courthouses designed by well-known Kansas architects and clearly intended to be "the symbol" of the community.

Railroads helped transform the architecture of Kansas by changing the relationship of time and space. No longer was Kansas isolated on the prairie. Kansas towns and cities became "metropolitan." The ability to travel quickly brought with it the sharing of ideas about community, culture, and commerce. Opera houses, banks, and elaborate mansions were the result of our growing economy.

I am proud of our architectural heritage, and I encourage you to explore the 8 Wonders of Kansas Architecture and the 16 finalists. They are the product of the people of Kansas who used their tools, materials, and ideas to create a unique architectural heritage that is worthy of praise. Explore and be inspired!

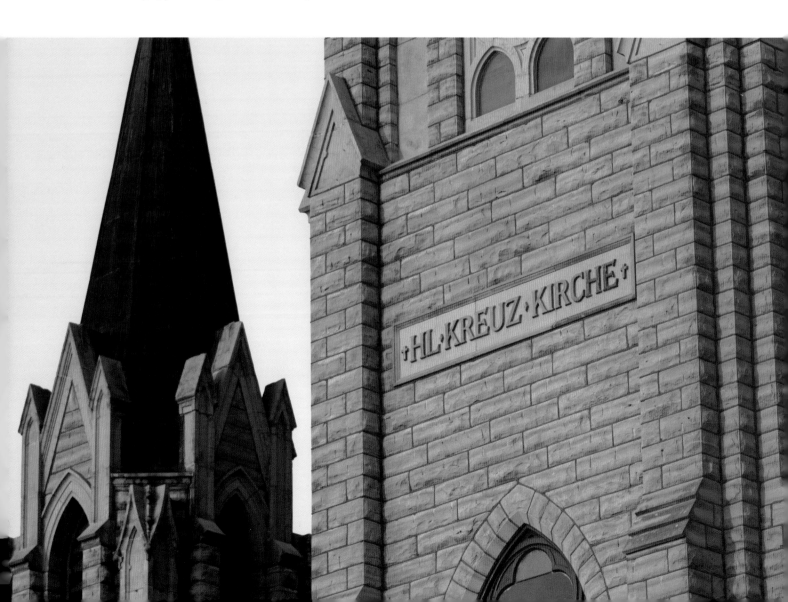

CHASE COUNTY COURTHOUSE, Cottonwood Falls

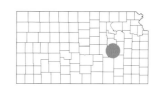

TOP 8 WONDER: *The Chase County Courthouse is one of the 8 Wonders of Kansas Architecture because its striking French Renaissance (Second Empire) style and red mansard roof make it one of the most recognizable buildings in Kansas.*

LOCATION
308 Broadway,
Cottonwood Falls
66845

CONTACTS
620.273.8469;
chasechamber@
sbcglobal.net

HOURS
Self-guided tours
Monday-Friday
8 a.m.-5 p.m.; guided
tours available most
weekends and
holidays 12-4 p.m.
Admission charge.

For more information,
see page 46.

Architecture

Completed in 1873, it is the oldest county courthouse in use in Kansas and second oldest in continuous use west of the Mississippi River.

The courthouse was designed by noted Kansas architect John G. Haskell of Lawrence. Born in Vermont, Haskell came to Kansas in 1857 at the age of 25 and soon rose to prominence as one of the state's leading architects. He was the first architect of the Kansas statehouse, and he designed many other important early Kansas buildings.

The French Renaissance (Second Empire) style is characterized by the roof's distinctive shape. Standing 113 feet tall, the courthouse and its red mansard roof are visible from vantage points

throughout the county. Featured within this limestone structure is a three-story spiral staircase made from walnut trees that grew along the Cottonwood River.

On the National Register of Historic Places, this Flint Hills icon received a $2.4 million renovation and restoration completed in 2008.

explorer extras...

The second oldest Kansas courthouse in continuous use is the 1884 Pottawatomie County courthouse, 106 Main, Westmoreland. The third oldest is the 1886 Linn County courthouse, 4th and Main, Mound City. Both buildings are open Monday-Friday 8:30 a.m.-4:30 p.m. **ee**

COOPER BARN, Colby

TOP 8 WONDER: *The Cooper Barn is one of the 8 Wonders of Kansas Architecture because it is purported to be the largest barn in Kansas and was one of the finest show cattle barns of its time.*

The grand barn is 66 feet wide, 114 feet long, and 48 feet high, and is topped with a gambrel roof. It was built at Breton, sixteen miles northeast of Colby, in 1936.

The imposing cattle barn was part of Foster Farms and housed as many as 75 head of prize-winning registered Hereford cattle. Under the management of Doc Mustoe, the farm became nationally recognized as a top Hereford breeder.

The barn's exterior incorporated attractive house siding, four openings in the loft floor allowed hay to drop to the runway below, and three six-foot-tall metal cupolas provided ventilation for the haymow.

In 1965 Foster Farms dissolved and the barn sold to a group that included Willard Cooper and his son Gary. In 1991 the Cooper family generously donated the landmark Cooper Barn to the Prairie Museum of Art and History in Colby. On May 15, 1992, the barn made the epic 16-mile journey to its present location, in the museum complex.

Inside the barn is an outstanding agricultural exhibit. Visitors to the Prairie Museum of Art and History may also tour the barn.

explorer extras...

The Prairie Museum of Art and History features artifacts collected from around the world by Joe and Nellie Kuska. For contacts and hours, see Cooper Barn. The impressive Charlie Norton bronze, Spirit of the Prairie, *stands near the entrance of the Thomas County courthouse, 300 N. Court, Colby.* **ee**

LOCATION
1905 S. Franklin,
Colby 67701

CONTACTS
785.460.4590;
prairiem@st-tel.net;
www.prairiemuseum.org

HOURS
Monday-Friday
9 a.m.-5 p.m.;
Saturday-Sunday
1-5 p.m.;
closed Mondays
November to April.
Admission charge.

FROMME-BIRNEY ROUND BARN, Mullinville

TOP 8 WONDER: *The Fromme-Birney Round Barn is one of the 8 Wonders of Kansas Architecture because of its rarity, quality, and beautifully restored condition.*

Out of the thousands of barns built in early Kansas, only 23 were round and few of them remain. In 1912 Henry Fromme hired William "Pat" Campbell to build a large round barn to house his Percheron horses. Round barns were promoted as more wind and cyclone resistant, an efficient use of space, and requiring less lumber to construct. The $8,000 cost was several thousand dollars higher than that of other barns of the time.

Not actually round, but 16 sided, the barn stands 50 feet tall and 70 feet in diameter. It is covered with a double-pitch, domical roof topped with a 16-sided cupola. Every rafter was cut with a hand saw using only a framing square to compute the angles necessary to make the 160 two-by-sixes converge on the cupola. A 16-sided granary stands in the center of the barn on the first floor.

In 1993 Phyllis Birney donated the barn to the Kiowa County Historical Society. It was listed on the National Register of Historic Places in 1987 and was restored to its original condition in 1995.

explorer extras...

Inside the Fromme-Birney barn are storyboards and photographs that explain the efficiency of round barns and relate the story of this structure and the family who owned it. At the barn's gift shop inside, visitors may buy an item simply by dropping the purchase amount in the container provided. Always open. **ee**

LOCATION
3½ miles south from U.S. 54 at Mullinville, then 1¾ miles west.

CONTACTS
620.548.2266;
neier1@cox.net;
http://skyways.lib.ks.us/orgs/barns/roundbarn

HOURS
Always open.
Donations welcome.

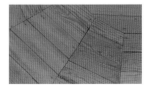

FROMME-BIRNEY BARN
HAS BEEN PLACED ON THE
NATIONAL REGISTER
OF HISTORIC PLACES
BY THE UNITED STATES
DEPARTMENT OF THE INTERIOR
CIRCA 1912 RESTORED 1995

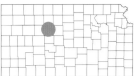

HOLY CROSS CHURCH, Pfeifer

TOP 8 WONDER: *Holy Cross Church is one of the 8 Wonders of Kansas Architecture because it is the finest example of a Gothic-style church in the state.*

Construction of the post-rock limestone church building began in 1915 under direction of Father Peter Burkard and was dedicated on May 3, 1918. Modeled after similar churches in Europe (especially Bavaria), Holy Cross features a rib-vaulted ceiling supported on delicate, decorative columns and pointed arches for the windows and doorways. The structure is 165 feet long, 50 feet wide at the nave, and 75 feet wide at the transepts. The central spire is 165 feet high and is believed to be the tallest Gothic church spire in Kansas. Each of the two side spires is 100 feet high. The stained-glass windows and additional interior decoration were added in later years.

Holy Cross is known as "the two-cent church" because parish families paid two cents for each bushel of wheat they produced to fund construction. Parishioners also donated much of the labor, including the quarrying and the stone delivery. The total construction cost was $56,000.

On July 1, 1993, the Diocese of Salina made the decision to dissolve the parish. However, the church itself remains open to the public on a daily basis and is in pristine condition.

LOCATION
10 miles south
of Victoria on
Pfeifer Avenue.

CONTACTS
785.735.2395

HOURS
Daily 8 a.m.-8 p.m.

explorer extras...
Many beautiful limestone churches can be seen in Ellis County and just beyond the county line. Visible from a distance, their tall spires lead you to Antonino, Catharine, Ellis, Gorham, Liebenthal, Loretta, Munjor, Schoenchen, Vincent, and Walker. Similar churches also are found in Hays. **ee**

KANSAS STATE CAPITOL, Topeka

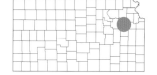

TOP 8 WONDER: *The Kansas State Capitol is one of the 8 Wonders of Kansas Architecture because it is a magnificent structure of French Renaissance design built to house the governmental bodies of the State of Kansas.*

Construction began in 1866, just five years after Kansas attained statehood. Thirty-seven years later, in 1903, the capitol was complete. One of the largest state capitols in the nation, its total cost was just over $3.2 million.

Architectural features in the senate chamber include the 28 copper columns, the ceiling of European renaissance design, and the round glass windows imported from France.

The house chamber features wainscoting made from Tennessee rose-gray marble and trimmed with white Italian marble. The inset panels in the wainscoting on the east and west walls consist of brocelian marble, Belgian black marble, and jasper, a variety of quartz.

The outer dome, covered with copper sheeting, extends approximately 75 feet above the inner dome, which is composed of glass panels.

Listed on the National Register of Historic Places in 1971, the state capitol is undergoing full restoration. This project, which began in 2001 and includes new construction, will be completed in 2012.

explorer extras...

Two Robert Merrell Gage sculptures, one of Lincoln and the other of a pioneer woman, enhance the statehouse grounds. Atop the capitol dome is Richard Bergen's 22-foot bronze of a Kansa Indian pointing his drawn bow toward the North Star. **ee**

LOCATION
300 SW 10th,
Topeka 66612

CONTACTS
785.296.3966;
capitol@kshs.org;
www.kshs.org/
portal_capitol

HOURS
Monday-Friday
8 a.m.-5:30 p.m.;
guided tours available
through the visitor
center, 785.296.3966.
Reservations
recommended.
Dome tours resume
in 2012.

LEBOLD MANSION, Abilene

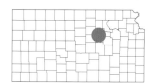

TOP 8 WONDER: *The Lebold Mansion is one of the 8 Wonders of Kansas Architecture because it is a rare surviving example of Italianate Tuscan Villa design.*

Most villas in the United States were constructed of wood in an L-shaped floor plan. The much rarer villa style, common in Italy, is made of stone and is cube shaped. Because the Lebold Mansion is built in the latter style, it is a rare architectural specimen not only to Kansas but to the entire United States.

One of the mansion's most interesting features is the architects' re-use of the Hersey stone dugout, over which the mansion was built in 1880 for banker Conrad Lebold. Architects used the stone dugout, built on this site in 1857, as the foundation to support the weight of the mansion's 65-foot stone tower.

Listed on the National Register of Historic Places in 1973, the Lebold Mansion was constructed of native Kansas limestone. The brown-toned face stones were quarried in Russell County, and the corner quoin blocks and the lintels over the doors and windows were quarried from white limestone in Ellis County. The Russell County limestone is notable as its brown-yellow hue can be found only in Kansas.

explorer extras...

While in Abilene, enjoy a 90-minute, 10-mile excursion train ride from Abilene to Enterprise on the Abilene & Smoky Valley Railroad. Take a seat in the 100-year-old coach or in the open-air observation car. Board at 200 S. 5th, Abilene; 785.263.1077; 785.263.2550; www.asvrr.org; May through October, Wednesday-Sunday 10 a.m. and 2 p.m. **ee**

LOCATION
106 N. Vine,
Abilene 67410

CONTACTS
785.263.2231;
director@abilencityhall.com

HOURS
The Lebold Mansion changed owners in 2010 and is no longer open for tours.

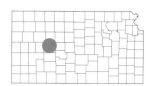

NESS COUNTY BANK, Ness City

TOP 8 WONDER: *Ness County Bank is one of the 8 Wonders of Kansas Architecture because of the building's hand-carved stone arches, rare extruded mortared joints, and beautiful interior woodwork.*

Said to be the finest and most imposing structure west of Topeka when it was completed in 1890, the four-story limestone bank was nicknamed the "Skyscraper of the Plains."

During the bank's construction, many Civil War veterans performed and oversaw such arduous tasks as hand carving and chiseling the stone and installing the woodwork. Ox carts carried the rock to town, and a block and tackle system was used to set the stone in place. One single stone in the arches weighed 6,820 pounds!

This impressive building contains 30 rooms and 13-foot pressed-tin ceilings, and it retains the original wainscoting, pocket doors, flooring, fireplaces, and front doors. The structure also boasts 110 high arched windows. According to the Ness County Bank Building Foundation, "The window fenestration is generally grouped in threes with second floor windows enclosed in enormous semi-circular arches which rise from the first floor line and provide a striking accent to the facade. The pyramid roof structure is flanked by four cut-stone spires."

The Ness County Bank building was listed on the National Register of Historic Places in 1972, and restoration and renovation ensued in the 1980s and 1990s. Currently the Ness County Chamber of Commerce occupies part of the main level, and the lower level houses Prairie Mercantile.

explorer extras...

Ness City's architectural highlights also include the decorative roundels that crown the parapet of each facade on the 1928 Ness County courthouse, 202 W. Sycamore, Ness City. The H.T. Holden bronze statue on the courthouse lawn is of Corporal Noah V.B. Ness, who served with the Seventh Kansas Cavalry during the Civil War. Ness County is the only Kansas county named for a corporal. **ee**

LOCATION
102 W. Main,
Ness City 67560

CONTACTS
785.798.2237;
785.798.2413;
nccofc@gbta.net;
www.nesscountychamber.com

HOURS
Tours available upon request; Ness County Chamber open Tuesday, Wednesday, Thursday 8-11 a.m.; Prairie Mercantile open Monday-Friday 1-5 p.m.

SEELYE MANSION, Abilene

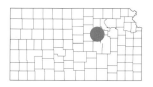

TOP 8 WONDER: *The Seelye Mansion is one of the 8 Wonders of Kansas Architecture because of the grandeur of this well-restored, three-story Georgian-style mansion.*

A New York architect designed this beautiful 25-room home in 1904 for Dr. A.B. Seelye, a patent medicine magnate, and his wife. The house is listed on the National Register of Historic Places and contains most of the original furniture and Edison light fixtures.

The Grand Hall fireplace is by Tiffany of New York, a hand-picked 1920 Steinway piano and a 1905 Edison Cylinder Phonograph grace the music room, and the dining room displays many pieces of glassware and other articles that belonged to Mrs. Seelye. During the Seelye family's occupancy, the "men" would, after dinner, traverse down the curved oak stairway to the bowling alley, one of many items in the home brought from the 1904 World's Fair. It is likely the oldest existing bowling alley in Kansas.

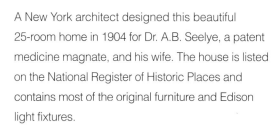

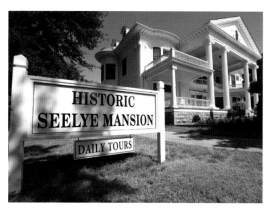

explorer extras...

Included in the tour, the Seelye Patent Medicine Museum contains many artifacts from the A.B. Seelye Medical Company, founded in 1890. Some of Seelye's cure-alls, such as Wasa-Tusa, Fro-zona, and Ner-vena, are on display. **ee**

LOCATION
1105 N. Buckeye,
Abilene 67410

CONTACTS
785.263.1084;
terryt@access-one.com;
www.seelyemansion.org

HOURS
Tours Monday-Saturday
10 a.m.-4 p.m.;
Sunday 1 p.m.-4 p.m.;
or by appointment.
Admission charge.

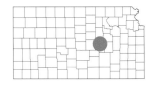

ADOBE HOUSE, Hillsboro

8 WONDER FINALIST: *Formerly known as the Peter Paul Loewen House, the Adobe House is a finalist for the 8 Wonders of Kansas Architecture because it is the last remaining immigrant Russian Mennonite clay-brick structure in North America.*

LOCATION
501 S. Ash,
Hillsboro 67063

CONTACTS
620.947.3775;
www.cityofhillsboro.net

HOURS
Saturday-Sunday
2-4 p.m.; or by
appointment; closed
January and February.
Admission charge.

Peter Paul Loewen and his family immigrated from a Mennonite colony in South Russia in 1876. That summer, Loewen built this unbaked-clay-brick house.

To construct the home, water, straw, and manure, trodden by horses, were mixed in a clay pit. This sticky substance was poured into brick molds of 4-by-6-by-12-inch compartments. A layer of mud served as plaster over which a coat of whitewash was added.

BROWN MANSION, Coffeyville

8 WONDER FINALIST: *The Brown Mansion is a finalist for the 8 Wonders of Kansas Architecture because of the original owner's relevance to regional history, and because of the home's grand Neoclassical style.*

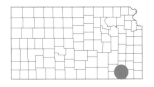

LOCATION
2019 S. Walnut,
Coffeyville 67337

CONTACTS
620.251.2550;
800.626.3357;
chamber@coffeyville.com;
www.brownmansion.com

HOURS
March to October,
Thursday-Tuesday
tours at 11 a.m., 1 p.m.
and 3 p.m.; November
to December, Saturday-
Sunday tours at 11 a.m.,
1 p.m. and 3 p.m.;
or by appointment.
Admission charge.

Having made a fortune in the natural gas industry, William Pitzer Brown built his 16-room mansion in 1906 for $125,000. First- and second-story verandas supported by Tuscan columns grace the south and west sides.

The mansion's "modern" conveniences included nine fireplaces (burning natural gas), gasoliers to illuminate the home, Tiffany leaded-glass panels, three full baths, and 20-inch-thick brick and concrete walls to insulate the gas heating system.

CHAPEL OF THE VETERANS, Leavenworth

8 WONDER FINALIST: *The Chapel of the Veterans is a finalist for the 8 Wonders of Kansas Architecture because of its ornate Gothic style, and because it is the only church where Protestant and Catholic religious services were conducted under one roof at the same time.*

Depicting religious and patriotic scenes, the stained-glass windows are visible from the upper-level Protestant chapel and from the lower-level Catholic chapel. Three gargoyles are found on the exterior. The tower has 11 tubular bells, but they are rarely used. The facility has been named a National Historic Landmark.

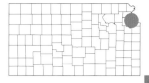

LOCATION
4101 S. 4th,
Leavenworth 66048

CONTACTS
913.758.6946

HOURS
Daily 8:30 a.m.-
4:30 p.m.

DYCHE HALL, Lawrence

8 WONDER FINALIST: *Dyche Hall is a finalist for the 8 Wonders of Kansas Architecture because of the beautiful carvings of birds, beasts, and reptiles that adorn this building, which houses the University of Kansas Natural History Museum.*

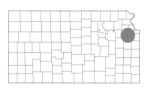

LOCATION
1345 Jayhawk
Boulevard,
Lawrence 66045

CONTACTS
785.864.4450;
naturalhistory@ku.edu;
www.nhm.ku.edu

HOURS
During the school year,
Monday-Saturday
9 a.m.-5 p.m.;
Sunday 12-5 p.m.
Admission charge.

This 1903 Venetian Romanesque limestone building is named for Lewis Lindsay Dyche, a naturalist, taxidermist, explorer, and KU professor. Its architectural style is characteristic of southern European churches of 1050-1200, and it is distinguished by a steep-roofed tower, arched doorway, and elaborate stone ornamentations of natural and fantastic animals and plants. Designed by Kansas City architects Walter C. Root and George W. Siemens, Dyche Hall was listed on the National Register of Historic Places in 1974.

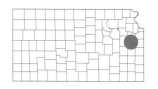

FRANKLIN COUNTY COURTHOUSE, Ottawa

8 WONDER FINALIST: *The Franklin County Courthouse is a finalist for the 8 Wonders of Kansas Architecture because it is the oldest surviving George P. Washburn courthouse in the state— and one of the most outstanding.*

LOCATION
315 S. Main,
Ottawa 66067

CONTACTS
785.242.1411;
barkerd@olddepot
museum.org

HOURS
Monday-Friday
8 a.m.-4:30 p.m.

The pride of Washburn's hometown of Ottawa, this 1893 structure was the second of 13 Kansas courthouses that the architect designed.

Listed on the National Register of Historic Places, this structure is a distinctive blend of two architectural styles: Romanesque Revival (round arches and unique sculptural program) and Colonial Revival (crisp red brick and white sandstone trim). Much of the interior, including the courtroom, remains original and in excellent condition.

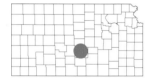

HISTORIC FOX THEATRE, Hutchinson

8 WONDER FINALIST: *The Historic Fox Theatre is a finalist for the 8 Wonders of Kansas Architecture because it is one of the finest examples of theatre Art Deco architecture in the Midwest.*

LOCATION
18 E. 1st,
Hutchinson 67501

CONTACTS
877.369.7469;
620.663.1981; thefox@
hutchinsonfox.com;
www.HutchinsonFox.com

HOURS
Monday-Friday
9 a.m.-5 p.m.;
guided tours available
with reservation.
Admission charge. See
www.hutchinsonfox.com
for performance and
movie schedule.

Built in 1931, the four-story theatre features impressive architectural detail including stepped terra cotta arches and capital blocks with floral and vegetable motifs, and pressed aluminum panels with geometric designs.

The marquee was the first flashing display of neon in Kansas and is one of the few surviving original and functioning marquees in the country. The Fox Theatre is listed on the National Register of Historic Places, and in 1994 it was named the State Movie Palace of Kansas.

OSBORNE COUNTY COURTHOUSE, Osborne

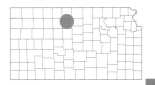

8 WONDER FINALIST: *The Osborne County Courthouse is a finalist for the 8 Wonders of Kansas Architecture because it is a shining example of Richardsonian Romanesque style and is renowned for the originality of its decorative interior.*

The Richardsonian Romanesque style is evident in the round-headed Romanesque arches and recessed entrances of this 1907 structure designed by J.C. Holland and Squires. Local building materials include Septarian concretion rock and post-rock limestone.

A carved lion's head and Medusa greet you at the entrance. The "face" of John Wineland, the sidewalk superintendent who irritated the stone masons, is integrated into the exterior of the south clock tower.

LOCATION
423 W. Main,
Osborne 67473

CONTACTS
785.346.2431;
obcoclerk@ruraltel.net

HOURS
Monday-Friday
8:30 a.m.-5 p.m.

ST. JOSEPH'S CATHOLIC CHURCH, Damar

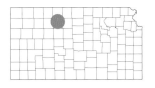

8 WONDER FINALIST: *St. Joseph's Catholic Church is a finalist for the 8 Wonders of Kansas Architecture because of its stunning interior, and because it is one of the best examples of a Romanesque Revival-style church in Kansas.*

LOCATION
107 N. Oak,
Damar 67632

CONTACTS
785.839.4343;
benoitt@ruraltel.net;
http://skyways.lib.ks.us/
towns/Damar

HOURS
During daylight.

The church has several unique construction features including cast concrete pillars and arches on the exterior and interior columns decorated with scagliola to appear like polished marble. The twin symmetrical square bell towers can be seen from miles away. Improvements added later include the beautiful stained-glass windows, interior decorating, and copper roof.

Father S.F. Guillaume directed the construction, F.A. Rothenberger was head stone mason, and Cidney Brown was head carpenter.

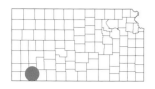

SAMSON OF THE CIMARRON, Seward County

8 WONDER FINALIST: *The Samson of the Cimarron railroad bridge is a finalist for the 8 Wonders of Kansas Architecture because it was considered a marvel in architecture, engineering, and construction when it was built in 1939.*

LOCATION
Between Liberal
(13 miles northeast
of Liberal on U.S. 54)
and Kismet in
Seward County

CONTACTS
620.626.0170;
tourism@cityofliberal.org;
www.cityofliberal.org

Following a long series of area railroad bridge collapses due to intermittent flooding, the Rock Island railroad built the "Mighty Samson" to cross the Cimarron River. At 1,268 feet, the colossal bridge is supported by four huge, art deco-style concrete pillars. The Samson replaced three and a half miles of curves and trestles and raised the railroad track 113-feet above the river bed.

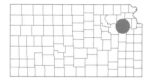

TOPEKA HIGH SCHOOL, Topeka

8 WONDER FINALIST: *Topeka High School is a finalist for the 8 Wonders of Kansas Architecture because its Gothic design makes it one of the most magnificent secondary schools in the Midwest.*

LOCATION
800 SW 10th,
Topeka 66612

CONTACTS
785.295.3200;
thshs2001@yahoo.com;
http://ths.topekapublic
schools.net

HOURS
Tours by appointment.

Built in 1931, its many outstanding features include a 165-foot main tower with a working Deagan Chimes system, a library modeled after Hampton Court Great Hall, a cafeteria with wood-beamed ceiling and wainscoting, an English classroom reminiscent of an Elizabethan withdrawing room, and Hoehner Auditorium illuminated by 10 massive chandeliers. The structure exhibits diverse architectural styles including Classical, Colonial, Tudor, Mediterranean, and Perpendicular Gothic.

The school is on the National Register of Historic Places.

WICHITA CARTHALITE, Wichita

8 WONDER FINALIST: *Wichita Carthalite is a finalist for the 8 Wonders of Kansas Architecture because it is a remarkable example of an indigenous and historic architectural innovation that, according to some architectural historians, may be unique to the United States.*

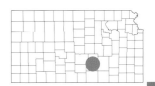

In the early 20th century, white and gray cast stone was a common building material. In the 1920s and 1930s the Cement Stone and Supply Company of Wichita adopted an unusual process to add color to its concrete by incorporating mineral pigments and crushed colored glass. As a result, beautifully colored designs could be applied to buildings' concrete surfaces. The product's brand name was Carthalite.

LOCATION

Carthalite structures in Wichita include Minisa Bridge, 2 blocks west of Waco and 13th; Kansas Aviation Museum, 3350 S. George Washington Boulevard; Dockum Drug Store building, 3200 E. Douglas; North Riverside Park Comfort Station, 1 block west of Nims and 9th; Allen's Market building, 2938 E. Douglas; and Griffin Architectural Office building, 416 S. Market.

WINDSOR HOTEL, Garden City

8 WONDER FINALIST: *The Windsor Hotel, currently under renovation, is a finalist for the 8 Wonders of Kansas Architecture because of its open atrium design, an innovative architectural feature in 1887.*

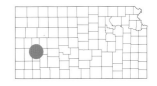

This four-story, 55,000-square-foot structure opened with 125 hotel rooms and a large dining room. Among the hotel's many elegant features, the atrium is its most impressive. Beginning on the second floor, it extends upward three stories and is topped with a vaulted skylight.

Known as the "Waldorf of the Prairies," the hotel represented opportunity and enterprise, and before the turn of the century, it was a headquarters for many heads of wealthy cattle firms.

LOCATION
Main and Pine,
Garden City 67846

CONTACTS
620.275.4340;
donharness@
sbcglobal.net;
www.gardencity.
net/windsor

HOURS
Tours by appointment.

wonders of Kansas!

Art Top 8 Wonders

Birger Sandzén, Lindsborg

Blackbear Bosin's *Keeper of the Plains*, Wichita

Blue Sky Sculpture, Newton

Charlie Norton's *Buffalo Bill* Bronze Sculpture, Oakley

Garden of Eden and Grassroots Art Mecca, Lucas

Gordon Parks, Fort Scott

John Steuart Curry Murals, Topeka

St. Mary's Catholic Church, St. Benedict

Art Finalist Wonders

Thomas Hart Benton's *Ballad of the Jealous Lover of Lone Green Valley*, Spencer Museum of Art, Lawrence

Boyer Museum of Animated Carvings, Belleville

Davis Memorial, Hiawatha

Do-Ho Suh's *Some/One*, Nerman Museum of Contemporary Art, Overland Park

Elizabeth "Grandma" Layton, Wellsville

Kansas Art Collection, Marianna Kistler Beach Museum of Art, Manhattan

Lester Raymer's Red Barn Studio, Lindsborg

M.T. Liggett's Metal Sculptures, Mullinville

Martin H. Bush Outdoor Sculpture Collection, Ulrich Museum of Art, Wichita

Pete Felten's Stone Sculptures, Hays and statewide

Poco Frazier's *Justice* Statue, Topeka

Post Office Section Art, statewide

Stan Herd Earthwork, Atchison

Tiffany Windows, Topeka

Tom Otterness's *Dreamers Awake*, Wichita Art Museum, Wichita

Wichita High School North Exterior Paintings, Wichita

By Jim Richardson, *National Geographic* photographer

That Kansas should be so rich in art is, for many, unexpected. Not for me. I grew up in this vast slate of a state and, after some years away, chose to return to it. Kansas is steeped in the space and quiet that give people with an artistic hankering the time to stew and brew, figure and dream. Art here comes from deep within our inner workings; sometimes it moves in fits like a thunderstorm. Kansas artists speak the language of the prairie soul.

If you are starting a tour of Kansas art, then I wish I could go along. What a journey to relish the sun-drenched roads to the works of our state's acknowledged artistic greats such as oil painter Birger Sandzén and photographer Gordon Parks. Or to stand before the monuments that are Blackbear Bosin's sculpture Keeper of the Plains *and our state capitol with its John Steuart Curry murals. I hope you'll lean in to inspect, like so many wildflowers, the lush details of St. Mary's Catholic Church and the hide of Charlie Norton's buffalo sculpture. Gaze up while standing inside the folk art canyon that is the Garden of Eden and before the gleaming face of Phil Epp's sculpture* Blue Sky.

There is so much more Kansas art to roam—more than even I know. This arts landscape can be fresh and unexpected—maybe even shocking. And it continues to emerge from a great wellspring within our people.

BIRGER SANDZÉN, Lindsborg

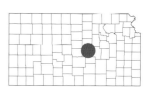

TOP 8 WONDER: *Birger Sandzén (1871-1954), born and raised in Sweden, is one of the 8 Wonders of Kansas Art because of his unique landscape paintings, which feature bold brushwork and vibrant color, and because of his fine lithographs, block prints, and dry points.*

Dr. Carl Aaron Swensson, founder of Bethany College in Lindsborg, offered Sandzén a position at the college in 1894. He remained there until retirement in 1946. Throughout his life, Sandzén was a prolific painter and printmaker completing more than 2,600 oil paintings and 500 watercolors.

Critics have praised and continue to praise Sandzén's work. Paris art critic Guiseppe Pelletieri wrote, "Birger Sandzén is the poet-painter of immense sun-washed spaces, of pine-crowned luminous, gigantic rocks, and of color-shifting desert sands. The spectator is amazed at this captured beauty. This dreamer-painter is truly a master."

The Birger Sandzén Memorial Gallery in Lindsborg showcases Sandzén's paintings, his prints, and his legacy as a painter, printmaker, and educator whose influence on the arts of Kansas and the nation is highly respected.

explorer extras...

Sandzén was a charter member of the Prairie Printmakers, a sizable collection of which can be seen at Coutts Memorial Museum of Art, 110 N. Main, El Dorado; 316.321.1212; www.couttsmuseum.org; Tuesday, Thursday 9 a.m.-5 p.m.; Wednesday, Friday, Saturday 1-4 p.m.

LOCATION
Birger Sandzén
Memorial Gallery,
401 N. 1st,
Lindsborg 67456

CONTACTS
785.227.2220;
fineart@sandzen.org;
www.sandzen.org

HOURS
Tuesday-Sunday
1-5 p.m. Donations
welcome.

Art

BLACKBEAR BOSIN'S *KEEPER OF THE PLAINS*, Wichita

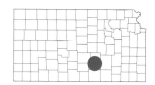

TOP 8 WONDER: Keeper of the Plains *is one of the 8 Wonders of Kansas Art because it is an awe-inspiring sculpture by well-known artist Blackbear Bosin that honors the region's original citizens and has become a symbol of Wichita.*

Art

The majestic 44-foot, five-ton *Keeper of the Plains* was designed by Blackbear Bosin (1921-1980), a Kiowa-Comanche and internationally recognized artist, muralist, and designer. The sculpture was Bosin's gift to the city of Wichita.

The colossal steel statue was placed at the confluence of the Little Arkansas and Arkansas Rivers, which is considered a sacred site by some Native Americans and was home to the Wichita tribe for many years. The ceremony to dedicate the sculpture as a Wichita bicentennial project was held on May 18, 1974.

Keeper of the Plains recently underwent a renovation and now rests atop a new 30-foot pedestal facing east to greet the rising sun. The renovated sculpture was dedicated on

May 18, 2007. The Keeper Plaza incorporates American Indian history and embodies a "sacred hoop" representing the four life elements: earth, air, fire, and water.

explorer extras...

The Keeper of the Plains *Ring of Fire burns nightly for 15 minutes (weather permitting). Daylight Savings Time 9 p.m.; Standard Time 7 p.m.* **ee**

LOCATION
650 N. Seneca,
Wichita 67203

CONTACTS
316.350.3340;
www.wichita.gov/
CityOffices/Culture/Keeper

HOURS
Daily 5 a.m.-midnight.

For more information,
see page 45.

BLUE SKY SCULPTURE, Newton

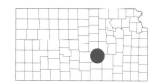

TOP 8 WONDER: *The* Blue Sky *Sculpture is one of the 8 Wonders of Kansas Art because it is a unique juxtaposition of sculptural imagery and natural sky, and because it provides the viewer with a heightened awareness of the changing Kansas sky.*

LOCATION
1500 N. Kansas
(in Centennial Park),
Newton 67114

CONTACTS
316.283.8027;
pepp@powwwer.net;
www.philepp.com/
public.htm

HOURS
Always open.

Art

This amazing sculpture, dedicated in 2001, was the joint effort of artists Phil Epp, painter and designer; Terry Corbett, ceramist and designer; and Conrad Snider, ceramist and designer.

To create *Blue Sky*, the drawing first was applied to brown paper with the same dimensions as the sculpture. The paper was then gridded, numbered, and cut into tile sizes. Corbett painstakingly transferred the paper patterns to the 1,600 tiles and individually glazed them. Finally, the stunning cobalt blue tiles were placed according to number on concrete.

The natural sky can be viewed behind the sculpture's gem-like surface and through the three-foot sky passageway. The fabricated blue sky and white cumulus clouds are quite dramatic in any weather condition.

Snider's large ceramic figures are intentionally abstract so that each observer can create an identity for them.

explorer extras...
A second Phil Epp and Terry Corbett blue sky tile sculpture stands outside Olathe's city hall, 100 W. Santa Fe. An Arlie Regier metal sculpture also adorns this pleasant courtyard. **ee**

CHARLIE NORTON'S *BUFFALO BILL* BRONZE SCULPTURE, Oakley

TOP 8 WONDER: *The* Buffalo Bill *Bronze Sculpture is one of the 8 Wonders of Kansas Art because it is a monumental work meticulously created by Kansas sculptor Charlie Norton and his wife, Pat, and is one of the world's largest bronze sculptures of Buffalo Bill.*

LOCATION
U.S. 83 and 2nd,
Oakley 67748

CONTACTS
785.671.1000;
info@buffalobill
oakley.org;
www.buffalobill
oakley.org

HOURS
Always open.

Art

The sculpture memorializes a legendary 1868 event in Logan County that resulted in William F. Cody winning the title "Buffalo Bill."

Norton's *Buffalo Bill* depicts Cody on his favorite horse, Brigham, taking aim with a Springfield rifle at a buffalo as both man and beast race across the prairie. This magnificent bronze is greater than two times life-sized and weighs over 9,000 pounds. The sculpture is historically correct in every detail, from the saddle and rifle to Cody's horse and the buffalo.

The Wild West Historical Foundation, Inc., a nonprofit corporation, was formed in 1999 to help make the *Buffalo Bill* sculpture a reality. The bronze was dedicated on May 22, 2004.

explorer extras...

While in Oakley, look for the impressive Spirit of the American Doughboy *statue outside the city office, 209 Hudson. This bronze sculpture, by Ernest Moore Viquesney, was dedicated in 1923.* **ee**

GARDEN OF EDEN AND GRASSROOTS ART MECCA, Lucas

TOP 8 WONDER: *The Garden of Eden and the Grassroots Art Mecca of Lucas share an entry as one of the 8 Wonders of Kansas Art because the Garden of Eden is one of the top ten contemporary folk art sites in the world, and because the Grassroots Art Mecca of Lucas comprises a unique art environment.*

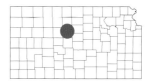

THE GARDEN OF EDEN

The Garden of Eden is a world-famous grassroots art site with one of the most fascinating (and bizarre) sculpture gardens in the world.

In 1905, at the age of 64, Civil War veteran Samuel Perry Dinsmoor began constructing this unusual site by building his home of limestone logs. Then, using 113 tons of cement, Dinsmoor built more than a dozen concrete trees to hold his 50 larger-than-life figures in his sculpture garden, which interprets his views of Populist politics, modern civilization, and the Bible.

While Dinsmoor was building and creating, locals tried to run him out of town. But the artist prevailed, and the Garden of Eden became the town's main attraction.

explorer extras...

See an "Open Range Zoo" in Lucas and along K-18 from Lucas east to the Lincoln/Ottawa county line. Artist Jim Dickerman makes his creatures from farm equipment, bikes, tools, and old car parts. 785.384.0616; www.wix.com/rainroxy/JRDs-Creature-Creations.
ee

LOCATION
Kansas and 2nd,
Lucas 67648

CONTACTS
785.525.6395;
lucascoc@wtciweb.com;
www.garden-of-eden-lucas-kansas.com

HOURS
May through October daily 10 a.m.-5 p.m.; November through February, Saturday-Sunday 1-4 p.m.; March through April daily 1-4 p.m. Admission charge.

For more information, see page 49.

Art

GRASSROOTS ART CENTER

Permanent visionary art environments exhibited here include Kansas artist Inez Marshall's brightly painted limestone sculptures; Ed Root's concrete, colored glass- and rock-embedded sculptures; and Herman Divers' life-sized motorcycle and car made from can pull tabs. Pieces by other self-taught artists are made from barbed wire, bones, chewing gum, and additional recycled materials. Outside, post-rock architecture and its artistry are displayed in the Post Rock Courtyard.

LOCATION 213 S. Main, Lucas 67648

CONTACTS 785.525.6118; grassroots@wtciweb.com; www.grassrootsart.net

HOURS May to September, Monday-Saturday 10 a.m.-5 p.m.; Sunday 1-5 p.m.; October to April, Monday, Thursday-Saturday 11 a.m.-4 p.m.; Sunday 1-4 p.m. Admission charge.

FLORENCE DEEBLE'S ROCK GARDEN

For more than 50 years Florence Deeble created "post card scenes" of her favorite vacation sites, including Mount Rushmore, by arranging and designing colored concrete and rocks in her backyard.

MRI-PILAR'S "GARDEN OF ISIS"

The walls and ceilings of seven rooms in the Deeble House are wrapped in silver insulation and mylar. Mri-Pilar has created an interior installation of over 2,000 3D sculptures made from recycled materials.

LOCATION Inquire at the Grassroots Art Center

CONTACTS 785.525.6118; www.grassrootsart.net

HOURS See Grassroots Art Center; tour included with Grassroots Art Center admission.

BOWL PLAZA (to open summer 2011)

Professional artists and volunteers created a replica of a gigantic white porcelain toilet bedazzled with mosaic designs on its exterior and interior walls to fill the bill, in Lucas fashion, for public restrooms.

LOCATION 121 S. Main, Lucas 67648

ERIC ABRAHAM'S FLYING PIG STUDIO AND GALLERY

World-famous artist Eric Abraham exhibits his fantastic ceramic creations that include porcelain flying animals and custom-designed mirrors with fairytale, biblical, and other themes. It is amazing and amusing art such as you've never seen before. Eric has studied art but he fits beautifully within this grassroots arts environment.

LOCATION 123 S. Main, Lucas 67648

CONTACTS 785.525.7722; eabraham@wtciweb.com; www.ericabraham.net

HOURS Irregular; contact Grassroots Art Center for admittance.

WORLD'S LARGEST SOUVENIR TRAVEL PLATE

Honoring the multiple "outsider art" environments that have flourished in Lucas, the World's Largest Souvenir Travel Plate depicts those environments along with a visual history of the town. The plate was designed by Erika Nelson, creator of the World's Largest Collection of the World's Smallest Versions of the World's Largest Things.

LOCATION ¼ mile south of 1st and K-18 intersection, Lucas 67648

CONTACTS 785.525.6377; info@worldslargestthings.com; www.worldslargestthings.com/kansas/travelplate.htm

HOURS Always open.

Gordon Parks
To Smile in Autumn

GORDON...
VOICES IN THE MIRROR
AN AUTOBIOGRAPHY

POETRY & IMAGES BY
GORDON PARKS

EYES WITH
WINGED THOUGHTS

GORDON PARKS, Fort Scott

TOP 8 WONDER: *Gordon Parks is one of the 8 Wonders of Kansas Art because of his world-renowned achievements in the arts including photography, filmmaking, writing, and music, which he attained during a time of racial barriers.*

Gordon Parks (1912-2006) wrote about his hometown of Fort Scott, Kansas, in his autobiographical novel and subsequent film *The Learning Tree*, which he also directed. He went on to direct additional films, author several books, and write original musical compositions, film scores, and a ballet.

He secured his reputation as a photojournalist by chronicling the Civil Rights movement for two decades in *Life* magazine. His work for *Vogue* established him as a master of fashion photography.

As a filmmaker, Parks was the first African American to direct a major Hollywood production, *The Learning Tree*, filmed on location in Fort Scott. He also broke new ground on the silver screen with a hip black hero named *Shaft*.

The Gordon Parks Museum and Center for Culture and Diversity focuses on the life and achievements of this great artist. The museum contains photos and memorabilia gifted by Mr. Parks.

explorer extras...

View more than 50 of Parks' signed photographs and 14 samples of his poetry in the public areas of Mercy Health Center, 401 Woodland Hills, Fort Scott; 620.223.7036; daily 7 a.m.-8 p.m. **ee**

LOCATION
Gordon Parks Center,
Fort Scott Community
College Academic Bldg.,
2108 S. Horton,
Fort Scott 66701

CONTACTS
800.874.3722, ext. 515;
gordonparkscenter@
fortscott.edu;
www.gordonparkscenter.org

HOURS
Monday-Friday
9 a.m.-5 p.m. during
the school year;
or by appointment.

JOHN STEUART CURRY
MURALS, Topeka

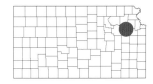

TOP 8 WONDER: *The John Steuart Curry murals are one of the 8 Wonders of Kansas Art because Curry was one of the greatest American Regionalist artists, and because he considered the state capitol murals his greatest work.*

In June 1937 John Steuart Curry, a native of Jefferson County, Kansas, was commissioned to paint murals in the Kansas statehouse. However, before he could finish, his work was criticized. As a result, Curry refused to sign and complete all that he had planned.

LOCATION
Kansas State Capitol, 300 SW 10th, Topeka 66612

CONTACTS
785.296.3966; capitol@kshs.org; www.kshs.org/ portal_capitol

HOURS
Monday-Friday 8 a.m.-5 p.m.; guided tours available at the Capitol Visitor Center.

For more information, see page 50.

Art

Tragic Prelude, the most famous of his finished murals, is the artist's interpretation of John Brown and the antislavery movement in Kansas Territory. Rich in symbolism, the painting depicts a fierce John Brown holding a Bible in one hand and a rifle in the other. Some accounts allege that Curry's critics disliked his color scheme and what they considered the mural's overall menacing effect. Some powerful politicians also objected to his proposed themes of dust storms, drought, and soil erosion for the final murals. They took steps that led to Curry refusing to finish his murals.

Lumen Martin Winter was hired to work from Curry's sketches and complete the murals, which he did in 1978.

explorer extras...
See a few of Curry's well-known works, pictures of his family, his paint brushes, books he illustrated, and more in his boyhood home, Old Jefferson Town, Oskaloosa; 785.863.3257; 785.863.2070; www.kansastravel.org/ oldjeffersontown.htm; May to September, Saturday-Sunday 1:30-5 p.m.; or by appointment. **ee**

ST. MARY'S CATHOLIC CHURCH, St. Benedict

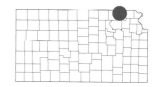

TOP 8 WONDER: *St. Mary's Catholic Church is one of the 8 Wonders of Kansas Art because of the grandeur of its lavish ornamentation, leaded windows, statuary, and murals. Additionally, it is the only known well-preserved church whose interior decor is by artist G.F. Satory.*

LOCATION
1 mile west of Seneca
on U.S. 36, 3 miles
north on K-178,
then ½ mile west.

CONTACTS
785.336.3174;
office@stmstb.org;
www.stmstb.org

HOURS
Daily 8 a.m.-5 p.m.

For more information,
see page 51.

Art

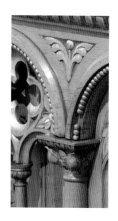

In contrast to St. Mary's rather simple 1894 limestone exterior, its award-winning interior presents awe-inspiring and intricate adornment. In 1901 Satory decorated St. Mary's with symbolic art by painting beautifully colored patterns, bands, and friezes on the walls, ceiling, cast iron columns, vault ribs, and window openings.

Adding to the interior's rich decor are 14 large oil paintings by Russian-born artist Th. Zukotynski, six Bavarian-made transept windows, and eight lead-glazed side windows consisting of two tall arched sections. In all, St. Mary's Church contains nearly 3,000 square feet of windows.

From 1980 to 1983 Joe Oswalt, a native of Waterville, Kansas, and a graduate of the Kansas City Art Institute, restored Satory's interior decoration and refurbished the oil paintings. In the early 1990s all leaded windows were rehabilitated by Hoefer Custom Stained Glass of South Hutchinson, Kansas. St. Mary's Church was placed on the National Register of Historic Places in 1980.

explorer extras...

Nemaha County is home to many outstanding churches. St. Bede's, a 1915 Gothic church, contains beautiful stained-glass windows from Munich (fine examples of 19th-century art), and the painted ceiling is breathtaking. Near Kelly, 5 miles east of Centralia on K-9, 1 mile north on K-63, then 1 mile east; watch for the single spire; open daily. **ee**

THOMAS HART BENTON'S *THE BALLAD OF THE JEALOUS LOVER . . .*, Spencer Art Museum, Lawrence

8 WONDER FINALIST: *Thomas Hart Benton's* The Ballad of the Jealous Lover of Lone Green Valley *is a finalist for the 8 Wonders of Kansas Art because it is a quintessential painting of an American scene, it is one of the artist's most representative pieces, and it is an outstanding example of Regionalism, an American art movement.*

LOCATION
1301 Mississippi,
Lawrence 66045

CONTACTS
785.864.4710;
spencerart@ku.edu;
www.spencerart.ku.edu

HOURS
Tuesday, Wednesday,
Friday, Saturday
10 a.m.-4 p.m.;
Thursday 10 a.m.-8 p.m.;
Sunday 1-4 p.m.;
hours subject to
change during holidays
and academic breaks.

In the painting, bands of color containing musical notes connect two seemingly unrelated scenes: in one, a man has stabbed his lover; in the other, a somber-faced trio of musicians gathers. The model for one of the musicians was Benton's friend and former student Jackson Pollock, an icon of the Abstract Expressionist movement. Benton painted what he knew best: rural midwestern life.

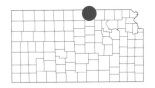

BOYER MUSEUM OF ANIMATED CARVINGS, Belleville

8 WONDER FINALIST: *The Boyer Museum of Animated Carvings is a finalist for the 8 Wonders of Kansas Art because of its more than 65 brilliant motion displays, including hand-carved figurines, created by Kansas artist Paul Boyer.*

LOCATION
1205 M,
Belleville 66935

CONTACTS
785.527.5884;
785.527.5524;
www.kansastravel.org/
boyergallery.htm

HOURS
Generally May
through September,
Wednesday-Saturday
1-5 p.m.; October
through April by
appointment.

Among these many fascinating and humorous creations are goats butting heads, men making wood shingles, and ball bearings riding on wire-track mazes and bouncing on drums.

If Boyer can visualize an idea, he can build it. Armed with a great imagination and a sense of humor, he hand carves and paints the figurines for his motion displays. He then shapes and bends each of the wire mechanisms to connect the figurines to the motors. The results are amazingly clever and entertaining.

DAVIS MEMORIAL, Hiawatha

8 WONDER FINALIST: *The Davis Memorial is a finalist for the 8 Wonders of Kansas Art because of its grandeur, and because of the controversy that surrounded this massive cemetery memorial.*

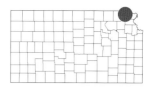

LOCATION
Mount Hope Cemetery,
½ mile east on Iowa
from U.S. 73
in Hiawatha

CONTACTS
785.742.7136;
hiawathachamber@
rainbowtel.net;
www.kansastravel.org/
davismemorial.htm

For more information,
see page 48.

Art

Initially it was a simple grave marker for John Davis' wife, Sarah, who died in 1930. But during the next seven years, Davis developed the site into a massive memorial that included 11 life-sized granite and marble statues. Many stories surround Davis' intent to build the lavish memorial including, thwarting his wife's heirs; refusing to underwrite a community hospital; and memorializing his wife.

The irony is that the Davis Memorial has benefited the community—every year thousands of visitors come to Mount Hope Cemetery to view the marble statuary.

DO-HO SUH'S *SOME/ONE*, Nerman Museum of Art, Overland Park

8 WONDER FINALIST: *Some/One by Do-Ho Suh is a finalist for the 8 Wonders of Kansas Art because the sculpture combines unexpected materials with universal themes and represents the diverse collection at the Nerman Museum, the region's largest contemporary art museum.*

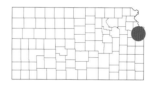

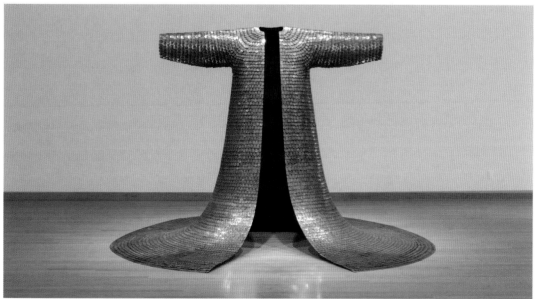

Courtesy of the Artist and Lehmann Maupin Gallery, New York

LOCATION
12345 College
Boulevard,
Overland Park 66210

CONTACTS
913.469.3000;
www.jccc.edu/museum

HOURS
Tuesday, Wednesday,
Thursday, Saturday
10 a.m.-5 p.m.;
Friday 10 a.m.-9 p.m.;
Sunday 12-5 p.m.;
closed during Johnson
County Community
College holidays.

Some/One, a 2004 work by Korean artist Do-Ho Suh, references hundreds of anonymous individuals united in collective conformity. Military dog tags are not memorials to individual soldiers, but rather to faceless troops. The hollow shell of armor reveals a blood-red velvet interior, inviting the viewer to visually step into the form and face mortality.

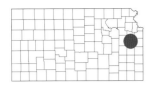

ELIZABETH "GRANDMA" LAYTON, Wellsville

8 WONDER FINALIST: *Elizabeth "Grandma" Layton is a finalist for the 8 Wonders of Kansas Art because the pencil and crayon drawings she began creating at the age of 68 resulted in more than 1,000 critically acclaimed images that addressed social issues.*

LOCATION
Wellsville Historical
Museum, 6th and Main,
Wellsville 66092

CONTACTS
785.883.4255;
crussell10@kc.rr.com;
www.elizabethlayton.com

HOURS
Saturday 9 a.m.-3 p.m.

Begun to offset her depression, Layton's work eventually not only cured her illness but changed the lives of many. Her art is known for its breadth, freshness, and expression of hope.

The Wellsville Library, 115 W. 6th, displays some of her work. Open Monday, Tuesday, Wednesday, and Friday 8:30 a.m.-5:30 p.m.; Saturday 8:30 a.m.-12:30 p.m.

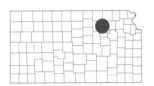

KANSAS ART COLLECTION, Beach Museum of Art, Manhattan

8 WONDER FINALIST: *The Kansas Art Collection at the Marianna Kistler Beach Museum of Art is a finalist for the 8 Wonders of Kansas Art because it is the largest and most diverse collection of its kind in Kansas.*

LOCATION
701 Beach Lane
at 14th and Anderson
(Kansas State
University campus),
Manhattan 66506

CONTACTS
785.532.7718;
beachart@ksu.edu;
www.beach.k-state.edu

HOURS
Wednesday-Saturday
10 a.m.-5 p.m.;
Sunday 12-5 p.m;
hours vary according
to KSU holidays;
tours available
with reservation.

With a mission to collect and care for the visual art of Kansas and the region, Beach Museum devotes the most gallery space in the state to exhibit the widest variety of Kansas art. It is a destination for those seeking to discover the state and its history through the eyes of scores of talented artists.

LESTER RAYMER'S RED BARN STUDIO, Lindsborg

8 WONDER FINALIST: *The Red Barn Studio is a finalist for the 8 Wonders of Kansas Art because it was the working studio of the late artist and craftsman Lester Raymer, and it exhibits his diverse works, many of which are made from recycled materials.*

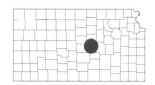

LOCATION
212 S. Main,
Lindsborg 67456

CONTACTS
785.227.2217; raymer@
redbarnstudio.org;
www.redbarnstudio.org

HOURS
Tuesday-Sunday 1- 4 p.m.;
or by appointment.
Donation welcome.

Art

The Red Barn Studio is filled with Raymer's art and handiwork including paintings, prints, ceramics, metalwork, woodcarvings, stitchery, furniture, and jewelry. His work is influenced by his love for the Southwest and Mexico, religious symbolism, folk art from all cultures, the world's great painters (especially the Spanish masters), and the circus. Raymer came to Lindsborg in 1946.

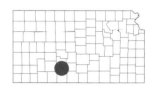

M.T. LIGGETT'S METAL SCULPTURES, Mullinville

8 WONDER FINALIST: *M.T. Liggett's metal sculptures are a finalist for the 8 Wonders of Kansas Art because these roadside signs and whirligigs are created in a fantastical nature to express political opinions.*

LOCATION
U.S. 400, just west of
Mullinville 67054

CONTACTS
www.roadsideamerica.
com/story/11212

Liggett traveled the world while in the military, but today he's in his shop converting his orneriness into sculpture. The results are lined along U.S. 400 west of Mullinville. There, hundreds of his totems and whirligigs appear in the shape of whimsical birds, demons, dragons, and bugs— all peculiar characters with idiosyncratic features. Made with welded and colorfully painted scrap iron and farm parts, many of these cartoonish metallic parodies carry inscriptions that are the latest word in political incorrectness.

101

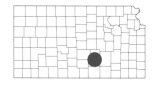

MARTIN H. BUSH OUTDOOR SCULPTURE COLLECTION,
Ulrich Museum of Art, Wichita

8 WONDER FINALIST: *The Martin H. Bush Outdoor Sculpture Collection, part of the Ulrich Museum of Art collection at Wichita State University, is a finalist for the 8 Wonders of Kansas Art because it has one of the most significant sculpture collections on a U.S. university campus.*

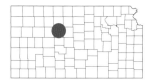

LOCATION
1845 Fairmount at
17th and Hillside
(Wichita State
University campus),
Wichita 67260

CONTACTS
316.978.3664;
ulrich@wichita.edu;
www.ulrich.wichita.edu

The outdoor collection, named for the founding director of the Ulrich Museum of Art, comprises 76 monumental works exhibited across the 330-acre WSU campus. Some of the works include Joan Miro's *Personnages Oiseaux*, Fernando Botero's *Woman with Umbrella*, and Tom Otterness's whimsical *Millipede*.

PETE FELTEN'S STONE SCULPTURES, Hays and statewide

8 WONDER FINALIST: *Pete Felten's stone sculptures are a finalist for the 8 Wonders of Kansas Art because many of them depict events and people representative of Kansas culture and history.*

LOCATION
Stone Gallery,
107 W. 6th,
Hays 67601

CONTACTS
785.625.7619.
Brochures with locations
of 22 Felten sculptures
in Hays are available
from 800.569.4505.

HOURS
Daily 10 a.m.-4 p.m.

A nationally known artist, Hays native, and self-taught sculptor, Felten has created numerous stone statues symbolic of the state's heritage. Among them are the Volga German immigrants (in Victoria), the pioneer family (in Oberlin), and *Monarch of the Plains,* an eight-by-ten-foot buffalo that stands on Fort Hays State University campus.

Felten's sculptures can be found throughout the Midwest, including his Four Famous Kansans, commissioned in 1981 and standing in the Kansas Capitol rotunda in Topeka.

POCO FRAZIER'S *JUSTICE*, Topeka

8 WONDER FINALIST: Justice, *an impressive sculpture inside the Kansas Judicial Center, is a finalist for the 8 Wonders of Kansas Art because of its elegance and singular symbolic portrayal of justice.*

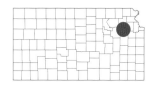

Designed by Bernard "Poco" Frazier, the 22-foot white marble statue departs from the traditional image of justice that depicts a woman, blindfolded, with sword and scales. Frazier's *Justice* offers a more gentle kneeling posture of a woman looking at her upraised arm, upon which is perched a prairie falcon symbolizing keen vision and swift, accurate action.

A native of Athol, Kansas, Frazier died before completing the sculpture. His son Malcolm, with Charles Gray and Dante Rossi, finished the seven-piece carving.

LOCATION
Kansas Judicial Center, 301 SW 10th, Topeka 66612

CONTACTS
785.296.2256; info@kscourts.org; www.kscourts.org/ kansas-courts/general- information/photo-album/ statue.asp

HOURS
Monday-Friday 8 a.m.-5 p.m.

Art

POST OFFICE SECTION ART, statewide

8 WONDER FINALIST: Post Office Section Art *is a finalist for the 8 Wonders of Kansas Art because of its purpose during the Great Depression to put Americans back to work, and because 27 original Kansas Post Office Art pieces remain today.*

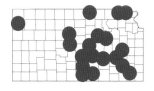

Unlike WPA art, Section Art was funded by the Section of Fine Arts in the U.S. Treasury Department. The "Section" selected high quality art to decorate public buildings thereby making it accessible to all people. The subject of each usually was based on the history or economy of the local community. Originally, 29 Section Art works adorned Kansas public buildings.

LOCATION
Section Art remains in the following 21 Kansas post offices: Anthony, Augusta, Belleville, Burlington, Caldwell, Council Grove, Eureka, Fredonia, Goodland, Halstead, Herington, Hoisington, Horton, Hutchinson, Kingman, Lindsborg, Neodesha, Oswego, Russell, Sabetha, and Seneca.

CONTACTS
For more about Section Art in the 21 post offices, and to find the locations of the other six existing pieces, go to www.8wonders.org.

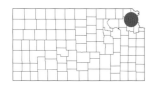

STAN HERD EARTHWORK, Atchison

8 WONDER FINALIST: *Stan Herd's Earthwork is a finalist for the 8 Wonders of Kansas Art because of the artist's exceptional ability to use the earth as his canvas and farm equipment as his brush.*

LOCATION
Amelia Earhart
Earthwork, Warnock
Lake, Atchison.
On K-73, south of
Atchison, turn right
on Patriot, immediately
left on Price (which
becomes 278th),
¼ mile south on 278th,
then ¾ mile west on
274th to Warnock Lake
entrance. Follow the
winding road to the
Earthwork platform.

CONTACTS
800.234.1854; tours@
atchisonkansas.net;
www.millermeiers.com/
stanherd

A native rural Kansan, Herd is nationally and internationally acclaimed for his field (crop) art in which he creates massive images on acres of land. He is considered the world's preeminent earthwork artist.

In Atchison, a 42,000-square-foot image of the world's most famous aviatrix, Amelia Earhart, was created from grasses, plants, earth, and stone. With help from community volunteers, Herd completed the earthwork in 1997.

TIFFANY WINDOWS, Topeka

8 WONDER FINALIST: *The Tiffany Windows in the First Presbyterian Church of Topeka are a finalist for the 8 Wonders of Kansas Art because they are Louis Comfort Tiffany originals installed in 1911, and because their exquisite colors are inherent in the glass.*

LOCATION
817 SW Harrison,
Topeka 66612

CONTACTS
785.233.9601;
info@fpctopeka.org;
www.fpctopeka.org

HOURS
Monday-Friday
9 a.m.-3:30 p.m.

With his knowledge of chemistry and glass production, the famous New York decorative artist created the remarkable iridescent colors of varied hues and shades within the glass itself rather than applying them to the glass. The resulting 10 windows in First Presbyterian are indescribably beautiful.

Tiffany came to Topeka to see the church before drawing any sketches. He planned the color scheme for the walls and skylights to harmonize with the completed windows.

TOM OTTERNESS'S *DREAMERS AWAKE,*
Wichita Art Museum, Wichita

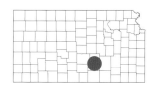

8 WONDER FINALIST: *Tom Otterness's* Dreamers Awake *is a finalist for the 8 Wonders of Kansas Art because the monumental bronze sculpture balances the artist's sense of humor with his desire to stimulate public dialogue about life and society.*

Dreamers Awake offers a view of two giant figures whose broken and fragmented bodies are overcome by chubby little characters. Intent upon making art about life's messy predicaments in defiance of modernist purity, Otterness identifies strongly with the so-called "outsider" artists, especially Samuel P. Dinsmoor of Garden of Eden fame.

Born in Wichita in 1952, Otterness is an internationally acclaimed artist. He completed *Dreamers Awake* in 1995.

LOCATION
1400 W. Museum Boulevard, Wichita 67203

CONTACTS
316.268.4921; info@wichitaartmuseum.org; www.wichitaart museum.org

HOURS
Tuesday-Saturday 10 a.m.-5 p.m.; Sunday 12-5 p.m. Admission charge.

Art

WICHITA HIGH SCHOOL NORTH EXTERIOR PAINTINGS, Wichita

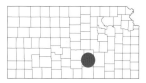

8 WONDER FINALIST: *Wichita High School North is a finalist for the 8 Wonders of Kansas Art because of the colorful bas-relief sculptures and decorative panels that adorn its exterior.*

Sculpted by Bruce Moore, the exterior decorations were integral to the school's architectural plans. Capturing the area's history, they tell a story of struggles between pioneers, Native Americans, and nature. A pioneer plowman with his yoke of oxen; a Native American chief, a scout, and a hunter; and buffaloes and eagles dominate the vignettes against the background hills and sun. The full-sized figures were fashioned by Terra Cotta Ornamental Works.

Bruce Moore, born in Bern, Kansas, in 1905, created the sculptures for Wichita North when it was constructed in 1929.

LOCATION
1437 N. Rochester, Wichita 67203

CONTACTS
316.973.6303; vjohnson1@usd259.net

Commerce Top 8 Wonders

Big Brutus, West Mineral

Brant's Meat Market, Lucas

Frontenac Bakery, Frontenac

Hemslöjd, Lindsborg

MarCon Pies, Washington

Moon Marble Company, Bonner Springs

Stafford County Flour Mills, Hudson

Vonada Stone Company, Sylvan Grove

Commerce Finalist Wonders

Baxter's Bait and Tackle, Stockton

Bowersock Mills and Power Company, Lawrence

Brookover Feed Yards, Garden City

Cloud Ceramics, Concordia

Cobalt Boats, Neodesha

Dessin Fournir, Plainville

El Dorado Oil Field, El Dorado

Koerperich Bookbinders, Selden

Mill Creek Antiques, Paxico

Millers of Claflin, Claflin

RANS, Hays

Ringneck Ranch, Tipton

The Grasshopper Company, Moundridge

Wichita Aviation Industry, Wichita

Winter Livestock, Dodge City

Wolf Creek Generating Station, Burlington

Josh Svaty, farmer and former Kansas Secretary of Agriculture

Czechs, Germans, Italians, Swedes, and more— the 8 Wonders of Kansas Commerce is a snapshot of the diverse ethnic heritage of our state. Immigrants arrived in Kansas looking for better opportunities for their families. In the process of providing goods and services for others they combined what they found in Kansas with individual history, placing an indelible mark of heritage on our commerce.

This tradition continues today. As new immigrant groups arrive, they bring with them their own cultures and the same entrepreneurial spirit that continues to shape the wonders of Kansas commerce. Discover your personal family history, and I promise you will find a business somewhere in Kansas that can immediately connect you to your pioneer generation that left their homes to make a new life in Kansas. For me it is Brant's Market in Lucas— a sample of homemade bologna and the good-natured banter that only a Czech could provide, and I'm home.

Perhaps the sesquicentennial lesson of Kansas commerce is that open skies and open communities are a good recipe for creating new businesses. As new people continue to flourish here, we will always see new wonders of Kansas commerce.

Commerce

BIG BRUTUS, West Mineral

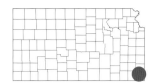

TOP 8 WONDER: *Big Brutus is one of the 8 Wonders of Kansas Commerce because it is the largest electric coal shovel in the world and, as a museum it represents the coal mining industry of southeast Kansas.*

LOCATION
6509 NW 60th,
West Mineral 66782.
7 miles north of
Columbus on K-7,
6 miles west on K-102,
and ½ mile south.

CONTACTS
620.827.6177;
bigbrutus@
columbus-ks.com;
www.bigbrutus.org

HOURS
January through March
daily 10 a.m.-4 p.m.;
April through May
daily 9 a.m.-5 p.m.;
Memorial Day to Labor
Day daily 9 a.m.-7 p.m.;
Labor Day to January
daily 9 a.m.-5 p.m.
Admission charge.

For more information,
see page 45.

Commerce

The black and orange, 160-foot-tall electric coal shovel can be seen from miles away. Designed and built by Bucyrus-Erie for the Pittsburg & Midway Coal Mining Company, the 1850-B coal shovel is the only one of its kind ever built and is recognized as an engineering accomplishment. It required 150 railroad cars to haul all the parts.

A three-man crew ran Big Brutus with the support of electricians and roller operators. It ran 24 hours a day, seven days a week from 1963 until 1974 at a speed of less than a quarter mile per hour, and it moved approximately one square mile each year. Big Brutus did not dig coal. The huge bucket removed the overburden (dirt and rocks covering the coal seams) and with one scoop could fill three railroad cars. Huge coal strippers moved in on the coal seams after Big Brutus exposed them.

explorer extras...
Big Brutus souvenirs and coal mining information, including exhibits and displays, can be found at the Big Brutus Visitors Center. The center also hosts special events and provides facilities for campers. **ee**

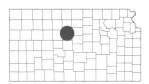

BRANT'S MEAT MARKET, Lucas

TOP 8 WONDER: *Brant's Meat Market is one of the 8 Wonders of Kansas Commerce because this family business, which started in 1922, cuts and prepares all of its meat products on site using a variety of old-fashioned methods.*

Commerce

Inside the small brown-brick building with big glass windows and awning, you'll find wall murals depicting the Brant's native land, Czechoslovakia, and a few grocery staples on the shelves. The brass cash register and original meat cooler confirm that you've come across a genuine throwback experience. Before you can rest your foot on the counter's brass rail, Doug Brant will be offering you a sample of his famous bologna or sausage.

Homemade meats start with Brant's bologna (a ring ready to eat) and continue on to include pepper sausage, smoked sausages, liverwurst, beef jerky, hamburger, steaks, dry-cured bacon, beef and pork roasts, and pork chops. Sage, salt, and pepper are added to the fresh ground sausage. A variety of delicious cheeses also is available.

explorer extras...

Brant's is a one-man operation. Doug does all the cutting, smoking, stuffing, grinding, selling, cleaning, opening, and closing— a busy man, but always glad to visit with customers. **ee**

LOCATION
125 S. Main,
Lucas 67648

CONTACTS
785.525.6464,
lucascoc@wtci.com

HOURS
Monday-Friday
8 a.m.-5:30 p.m.;
Saturday
8 a.m.-5:30 p.m.

FRONTENAC BAKERY, Frontenac

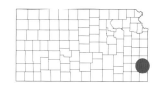

TOP 8 WONDER: *Frontenac Bakery is one of the 8 Wonders of Kansas Commerce because it has operated for more than 100 years in the same location, and because it continues to use the original recipes and original giant oven.*

LOCATION
211 N. Crawford,
Frontenac 66763

CONTACTS
620.231.7980
for group tours;
hite@ckt.net

Commerce

George Vacca, an Italian immigrant, came to southeast Kansas in the late 1800s to work in the coal mines. Having been a baker in northern Italy, he resumed this vocation after injuring his knee in a mining accident. Thus, in 1900 Frontenac Bakery was established. Brian and JoLynn Hite bought the business in 2007 and continue operating it today.

The giant oven, which dates to the bakery's founding, is constructed of brick surrounded by sand, which keeps the temperature inside at an even 425 degrees Fahrenheit.

Frontenac Bakery provides 500 to 700 loaves of bread daily to all six chicken restaurants in Crawford County and Jim's Steakhouse in Pittsburg. Additionally, it makes bread crumbs, which are packed into 100-pound bags and sold to the chicken restaurants.

The bakery's product line also includes breadsticks, dinner rolls, and cinnamon rolls. And it uses flour that is grown, harvested, and milled in Kansas.

explorer extras...
Pallucca's Market, a 100-year-old Italian grocery store and deli, stocks Frontenac Bakery bread, cinnamon rolls, and non-bakery products including great selections of imported foods and olive oil, dry noodles, fresh spaghetti sauce, and Italian sausage made on site. 207 E. McKay, Frontenac; 620.231.7700; daily 9 a.m.-6 p.m. **ee**

113

HEMSLÖJD, Lindsborg

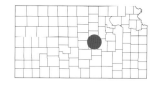

TOP 8 WONDER: *Hemslöjd is one of the 8 Wonders of Kansas Commerce because it is the only shop in the United States that handcrafts Dala horse-shaped signs and other traditional Swedish crafts. Furthermore, it is an international tourist site and has the leading Swedish gift catalog and Web site in the country.*

LOCATION
201 N. Main,
Lindsborg 67546

CONTACTS
785.227.2983;
swedes@hemslojd.com;
www.hemslojd.com

HOURS
Monday-Saturday
9 a.m.-5 p.m.
(7:30 p.m. in summer);
Sunday 12:30-5 p.m.;
closed Thanksgiving,
Christmas, and
New Year's Day.

Commerce

"Hemslöjd" is Swedish for handicraft. Throughout Sweden small hemslöjd shops have for generations crafted and sold products made of wood, textiles, and other materials. In 1984 Ken Sjogren and Ken Swisher established Hemslöjd in Lindsborg to continue this tradition in America. Hemslöjd's products include personalized wood Dala horse signs and Swedish-style door harps, clocks, candleholders, and custom-etched glassware.

Visitors are welcome to watch and visit with the craftsmen and women as they cut out, sand, assemble, and paint or decorate in the workshop. Monday through Saturday, customers will usually find at least one person at work.

In addition to crafting Swedish products, Hemslöjd also promotes Swedish heritage in America.

explorer extras...
Near Hemslöjd, Small World Gallery is a delightful open-space shop featuring the work of National Geographic *photographer Jim Richardson and the beautiful handcrafted jewelry of his wife, Kathy. 127 N. Main; 785.227.4442; www.smallworldgallery.net; Tuesday-Saturday 10 a.m.-5 p.m.; Sunday 12-3 p.m.* **ee**

MARCON PIES, Washington

TOP 8 WONDER: *MarCon Pies is one of the 8 Wonders of Kansas Commerce because it produces 500 to 1,500 pies daily, each made by hand using fresh and health-conscious ingredients.*

MarCon Pies began more than 25 years ago in the kitchens of Marilyn Hanshaw and Connie Allen, thus the company's name, MarCon. They began baking pies for auction lunch stands and developed a local pie delivery route. Today fresh baked, fresh baked then frozen, and unbaked frozen pies are made Monday through Friday and delivered to more than 100 eateries and supermarkets in Kansas, Nebraska, and Missouri.

Current owner Don Walsh has maintained MarCon's high quality and product diversity. More than 90 varieties of fruit, nut, and creme pies are available as well as a large assortment of cheesecakes. The pie crust, which uses cholesterol-free canola oil, was adapted from a family recipe and is exceptionally tender and flaky. Sugar-free pies made with sucralose are available in fruit, custards, and cremes and are becoming very popular.

Special orders, quick delivery (to ensure freshness), and the famous crust are only a few of MarCon Pies notable characteristics. Each pie maker has created a signature crimping style, and each crust is made with pride.

LOCATION
124 W. 8th,
Washington 66968

CONTACTS
785.325.2439;
marconpies@
sbcglobal.net;
www.marconpies.com

HOURS
Monday-Friday
8 a.m.-5 p.m.
Tours by reservation.

Commerce

explorer extras...
Gooseberry, strawberry, and strawberry-rhubarb pies may be hard to find, but these two-crust specialties are regulars on the MarCon Pie shelves. **ee**

MOON MARBLE COMPANY, Bonner Springs

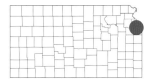

TOP 8 WONDER: *Moon Marble Company is one of the 8 Wonders of Kansas Commerce because it is the only store in Kansas, and one of the few in the United States, where you can buy handmade marbles and watch them being made.*

LOCATION
600 E. Front,
Bonner Springs 66012.
At the intersection of
K-32 and K-7.

CONTACTS
913.441.1432;
888.410.0680;
email@moonmarble.com;
www.moonmarble.com

HOURS
Tuesday-Saturday
10 a.m.-5 p.m.

Commerce

With your first step inside, you'll feel you've gone back in time. No matter your age, you'll likely find the shelves stocked with games or toys from your childhood.

A maker of wooden toys for many years, Bruce Breslow was always on the lookout for marbles to use with his game boards and marble runs. The difficulty in finding specialty marbles led to him opening the Moon Marble Company in 1997.

As visitors watch from bleachers, Breslow demonstrates the art of marble making. As he works, he provides marble history and other fascinating marble tidbits.

Breslow's handmade marbles are incredibly artistic and come in a multitude of unusual designs, shapes, and themes. Also available are machine-made marbles in all colors and sizes, from pee-wees to toebreakers (two-inch).

Moon Marble is a unique experience and a great place for fun—for any age. Call ahead for demonstration times and to arrange a field trip.

explorer extras...

Another Bonner Springs attraction, the National Agricultural Center and Hall of Fame presents a vast array of artifacts, exhibits, hands-on experiences, and more to help audiences understand and appreciate the importance of agriculture. The Hall of Fame honors those who have made significant contributions to agriculture. 630 Hall of Fame Drive, just north of I-70 and K-7; 913.721.1075; www.aghalloffame.com; April to October, Tuesday-Saturday 10 a.m.-4 p.m.; Sunday 1-4 p.m.; closed major holidays. **ee**

STAFFORD COUNTY FLOUR MILLS, Hudson

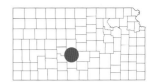

TOP 8 WONDER: *Stafford County Flour Mills is one of the 8 Wonders of Kansas Commerce because it is one of the last independent flour mills in the United States, and because it specializes in producing flour for the home baker.*

LOCATION
108 S. Church,
Hudson 67545

CONTACTS
620.458.4111;
customerservice@stafford
countyflourmills.com;
www.hudsoncream.com

HOURS
Monday-Friday
8 a.m.-5 p.m.;
Saturday 8 a.m.-12 p.m.;
group tours available
with reservations.

Commerce

In 1904 Gustav Krug and his brother-in-law Otto Sondregger founded Hudson Milling Company, later renamed Stafford County Flour Mills. The Krug descendants retained ownership until 1986 when the last Krug retired and no other family members remained. Hudson citizens, concerned about the mill's future, purchased controlling interest in it, and, as a result, Stafford County Flour Mills remained a locally owned company.

The mill has been perfecting the fine art of flour milling in the slow, traditional way for more than 100 years. Hudson Cream Flour (bleached) is the signature short-patent flour. To produce it, the wheat is ground more times than for other flours, and fine-meshed sieves sift away more by-products, leaving only the heart of the wheat kernel. Used as all-purpose flour, Hudson Cream produces baked goods with a light texture like no other flour can.

explorer extras...

Hudson is also home to the Wheatland Cafe. It's worth the drive to experience the Sunday buffet, which offers pan-fried chicken, bone-in ham, real mashed potatoes, homemade bread, homemade ice cream, and many other temptations. 112 N. Main; 620.458.4761; Sunday 11 a.m.-2 p.m. **ee**

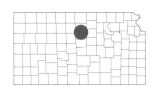

VONADA STONE COMPANY,
Sylvan Grove

TOP 8 WONDER: *Vonada Stone Company is one of the 8 Wonders of Kansas Commerce because it uses the old-fashioned feathers and wedge system to remove post rock from the earth, and because it carves the rock free hand using only antique tools.*

The company was founded in 1986 by the Vonada family: Duane, Donna, Damon, and Janet. Not only is it located in the heart of "post rock country" in the Smoky Hills, it is also on a third-generation working family farm.

Few stone companies other than Vonada break out Greenhorn Limestone with the feathers and wedge system, which is how it must be done to preserve the stone's natural look and include the fossils.

Group tours are available for those wishing to see how the stone is quarried using tools from 100 years ago. Tours are also given to those interested in learning how the stone is carved and in watching the 100-year-old vertical mill turn out post-rock bird baths, sundial mounts, benches, signs, and more. Visitors, by appointment, may also come to the shop to see the stone artwork for sale. Stone work and tours are intermittent as the Vonadas must also operate their farm and ranch.

explorer extras...
A historical marker tells the story of the South Fork Spillman Creek bridge, a 1908 double-arch stone bridge. The crossing served as a meeting place for three different ethnic groups. 8 miles north of K-18 on K-181 near Sylvan Grove. To view the stone bridge, park just north of the creek's new bridge. **ee**

LOCATION
540 E. Quail Lane, Sylvan Grove 67481. 6½ miles north of Sylvan Grove on K-181 to Quail Lane, then ½ mile west.

CONTACTS
785.526.7391;
785.658.7889

HOURS
Tours and visits by appointment only.

Commerce

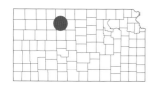

BAXTER'S BAIT AND TACKLE, Stockton

8 WONDER FINALIST: *Baxter's Bait and Tackle is a finalist for the 8 Wonders of Kansas Commerce because, known as "Little Cabela's," it maintains an unusually large inventory for a small-town store.*

LOCATION
424 Main,
Stockton 67669

CONTACTS
785.425.6321

HOURS
Daily 7 a.m.-7 p.m.

Starting the business to provide summer jobs for their five children, Blaine and Diane Baxter "forgot to close" after the kids graduated from school. Open every day of the year, Baxter's Bait and Tackle is an anchor on Main Street, bringing some big spenders to downtown—a priceless value to a town of 1,500. Its presence is very helpful to area outfitters who cater to nonresident hunters.

Old-time outdoor gear is displayed on shelves around the top of the room.

BOWERSOCK MILLS AND POWER COMPANY, Lawrence

8 WONDER FINALIST: *Bowersock Mills and Power Company is a finalist for the 8 Wonders of Kansas Commerce because it is the only operating hydroelectric plant in Kansas, and it has been continuously producing clean, renewable energy since 1874.*

LOCATION
546 Massachusetts,
Kansas River at the
Massachusetts
Street bridge,
Lawrence 66044

CONTACTS
785.843.1385;
staff@bowersockpower.com;
www.bowersockpower.com

HOURS
Tours by appointment.

A part of the flood control system of the Bowersock Dam, the baffles can be raised or lowered to control the amount of water that flows over the dam or is diverted to the power plant.

During the past 130-plus years, the mill has ground grain into flour, produced the first ready made gingerbread cake mix, hosted a radio station, operated as a paper mill, made barbed wire, and produced power.

BROOKOVER FEED YARDS, Garden City

8 WONDER FINALIST: *Brookover Feed Yards is a finalist for the 8 Wonders of Kansas Commerce because in 1951 it was the first commercial feed yard in the Midwest and remains an industry leader today.*

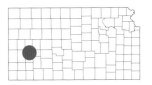

Earl Brookover envisioned that the irrigated High Plains, with its grain potential and moderate climate, would be ideal to meet the emerging demand for commercial cattle feeding. His vision held true, and today Brookover Feed Yards, still family owned, consistently feeds more cattle than any commercial feeder in the nation.

LOCATION
31013 N. U.S. 83,
Garden City 67846

CONTACTS
620.276.6662;
www.brookover.com

HOURS
Tours by appointment.
Learn more about
Earl Brookover and the
pioneering of the first
commercial feedlot at
the Finney County
Historical Museum,
403 S. 4th, Garden City;
620.272.3664.

Commerce

CLOUD CERAMICS, Concordia

8 WONDER FINALIST: *Cloud Ceramics is a finalist for the 8 Wonders of Kansas Commerce because it produces nearly 8 million top-quality bricks per month, earning a reputation as the "Cadillac" of brick lines.*

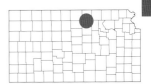

In 1944, after learning of clay outcroppings southeast of Concordia, Charles S. Cook tested the area and discovered a large deposit of Dakota clay suitable for manufacturing-quality building brick. In 1946 brick production began using 10 "beehive" kilns producing a half million bricks per month. Today Cloud Ceramics manufactures more than 30 different colors, sizes, and textures of brick from five different colors of clay from the same Dakota clay field.

LOCATION
1716 Quail Road,
Concordia 66901

CONTACTS
785.243.1284;
info@cloudceramics.com;
www.cloudceramics.com

HOURS
Tours by appointment.
Cloud County Museum
Annex also has a Cloud
Ceramics display.
130 E. 6th, Concordia;
785.243.1284.

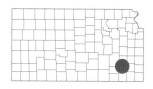

COBALT BOATS, Neodesha

8 WONDER FINALIST: *Cobalt Boats is a finalist for the 8 Wonders of Kansas Commerce because it is a leading manufacturer of luxury power boats with world-class marine design and manufacturing capabilities.*

LOCATION
1715 N. 8th,
Neodesha 66757

CONTACTS
800.468.5764;
www.cobaltboats.com

HOURS
Tours by appointment.

In 1968 Pack St. Clair founded a boat manufacturing company in land-locked Wilson County. Known for crafting the entire boat, from electrical systems to the upholstery, Cobalt Boats is still family-owned with an excellent reputation for customer satisfaction.

DESSIN FOURNIR, Plainville

8 WONDER FINALIST: *Dessin Fournir is a finalist for the 8 Wonders of Kansas Commerce because this luxury goods firm competes internationally from its rural Kansas headquarters.*

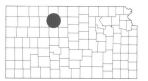

LOCATION
308 W. Mill,
Plainville 67663

CONTACTS
785.434.2777;
info@dessinfournir.com;
www.dessinfournir.com

HOURS
Tours by appointment.

The term Dessin Fournir is French and loosely translates as "to design" and "to furnish."

Pursuing his life-long passion for exquisitely designed, beautifully handcrafted home furnishings, Chuck Comeau co-founded the Dessin Fournir Companies in 1993. This nationally acclaimed firm targets high-end residential and contract markets. A design industry powerhouse with six companies that design and manufacture furniture, textiles, lighting, and wallpaper, its products are distributed in 14 national showrooms and in Toronto and Moscow.

EL DORADO OIL FIELD, El Dorado

8 WONDER FINALIST: *The El Dorado Oil Field is a finalist for the 8 Wonders of Kansas Commerce because the scientific methods used to discover this oil field changed petroleum exploration technology forever.*

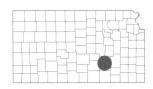

Few events in oil history—that is, the discovery of the El Dorado Oil Field—had such lasting effects on petroleum technology, the course of world events, and the economy. Stapleton #1, the 1915 discovery well, became the most notable in the region. Through unprecedented pinpointing, oil was found on nearly every acre of the geologists recommended area. As a result, refineries sprang up, support businesses thrived, and the aviation industry was launched.

To visit Stapleton #1 and its historical marker, follow the signs on N. Haverhill or 6th.

LOCATION
Kansas Oil Museum,
383 E. Central,
El Dorado 67042

CONTACTS
316.321.9333;
history@kansasoil
museum.org;
www.kansasoil
museum.org

HOURS
May to September,
Monday-Saturday
9 a.m.-5 p.m.; October
to April, Tuesday-Friday
9 a.m.-5 p.m.;
Saturday 12-5 p.m.
Admission charge.

Commerce

KOERPERICH BOOKBINDERS, Selden

8 WONDER FINALIST: *Koerperich Bookbinders is a finalist for the 8 Wonders of Kansas Commerce because it is one of the few binderies in the nation that still meets or exceeds Library Binding Institute specifications.*

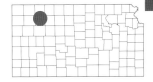

A small, family-run business in the rural town of Selden (population 190), Koerperich has steadily grown since its founding in 1969. Serving customers from coast to coast, the company takes great pride in the quality of its work. It specializes in short-run productions and uses sewing machines (instead of glue) to assure a durable book. Koerperich handles genealogy books, Bible restoration, school annual covers, and more.

LOCATION
104 N. Kansas,
Selden 67757

CONTACTS
785.386.4392;
kbindery@ruraltel.net;
www.kbindery.com

HOURS
Monday-Friday
7 a.m.-3:30 p.m.;
tours by appointment.

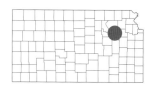

MILL CREEK ANTIQUES, Paxico

8 WONDER FINALIST: *Mill Creek Antiques is a finalist for the 8 Wonders of Kansas Commerce because it is the largest antique stove restoration business in the Midwest, and it anchored the comeback of Paxico.*

LOCATION
109 Newbury,
Paxico 66526

CONTACTS
785.636.5520;
stoveking@
millcreekantiques.com;
www.millcreek
antiques.com

HOURS
Monday-Saturday
9 a.m.-5 p.m.; Sunday
by appointment.

Steve Hund's love affair with wood stoves began in the 1970s in a house with no heat. His passion has grown into a thriving nationwide business. Hund restores rusty and broken wood and gas stoves into fully working and beautiful reminders of the past. The process includes disassembling, resealing, cleaning, polishing, replacing parts, and nickel-plating. Hund offers an extensive selection of antique stoves for sale.

A large variety of antiques are for sale at Mill Creek Antiques and other shops in Paxico.

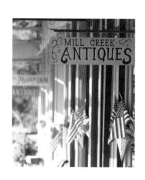

MILLERS OF CLAFLIN, Claflin

8 WONDER FINALIST: *Millers of Claflin is a finalist for the 8 Wonders of Kansas Commerce because it is the oldest and largest family-owned home furnishings store in Kansas and has created a colorful and historic presence downtown.*

LOCATION
200 Main,
Claflin 67525

CONTACTS
620.587.3601;
info@millersofclaflin.com;
www.millersofclaflin.com

HOURS
Monday, Thursday
9 a.m.-8 p.m.; Tuesday,
Wednesday, Friday
9 a.m.-5:30 p.m.;
Saturday 9 a.m.-5 p.m.

Picturesque buildings that serve as the 13 Miller showcase rooms or warehouses resemble the historic businesses that once graced downtown Claflin, population 690. Founded in 1903 by J.W. Miller, Millers of Claflin originally carried furniture, buggies, hardware, implements, and even windmills. Today this fifth-generation business has the largest furniture showroom, exceeding 80,000 square feet, in central Kansas.

RANS, Hays

8 WONDER FINALIST: *RANS is a finalist for the 8 Wonders of Kansas Commerce because it is a world leader in the ever-growing recumbent bike and kit plane industries.*

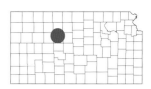

LOCATION
4600 U.S. 183 Alt.,
Hays 67601

CONTACTS
785.625.6346;
rans@rans.com;
www.rans.com

HOURS
Monday-Friday
8 a.m.-5 p.m.

Commerce

Established in 1974 by Randy Schlitter, RANS sets the standard for innovation using cutting edge technology to produce safe, high quality aircraft and bicycles. Hi-tech machines, known for accuracy and quality of cut, build precise parts for fast assembly. Fifty full-time employees, working with raw materials, create aircraft (both fly away and kits) and bicycles. Production planes and prototypes share the assembly hall, along with static test equipment and bike assembly.

RINGNECK RANCH, Tipton

8 WONDER FINALIST: *Ringneck Ranch is a finalist for the 8 Wonders of Kansas Commerce because it offers exceptional upland game bird hunting and is a prime example of rural entrepreneurship utilizing natural resources.*

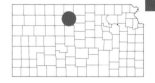

LOCATION
655 Solomon Road,
Tipton 67485

CONTACTS
785.373.4835; debra@
ringneckranch.net;
www.ringneckranch.net

Five generations of Houghtons have built the ranch, homesteaded in 1872, into an outstanding example of the state's ranching industry. A hunting lodge operation since 1983, the ranch offers 10,000 acres of exceptional upland game bird hunting of several species, particularly the wily Ringneck pheasant. Ringneck Ranch, in the Blue Hills of north-central Kansas, is also a national destination for company retreats.

THE GRASSHOPPER COMPANY, Moundridge

8 WONDER FINALIST: *The Grasshopper Company is a finalist for the 8 Wonders of Kansas Commerce because it introduced the first commercially viable zero-turn mower in the United States and maintains a worldwide market.*

LOCATION
105 Old U.S. Hwy. 81,
Moundridge 67107

CONTACTS
620.345.8621; info@
grasshoppermower.com;
www.grasshopper
mower.com

HOURS
Tours by appointment.

A family business since 1969, Grasshopper introduced many "firsts" in the zero-turn mower industry, including the first dual swing-away control levers (1973), the first liquid-cooled diesel engine in a zero-turn radius mower (1984), and a mower deck that raises upright with the flip of a switch (2004).

More than 300 employees proudly build commercial mowers and grounds maintenance equipment in the state-of-the-art manufacturing facility that incorporates robots and computer-controlled processes.

WICHITA AVIATION INDUSTRY, Wichita

8 WONDER FINALIST: *The Wichita Aviation Industry is a finalist for the 8 Wonders of Kansas Commerce because the "Air Capital of the World" manufactures more than half of the world's general aviation light aircraft and business jets, and it is a major supplier to the builders of commercial airliners.*

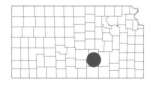

LOCATION
Kansas Aviation
Museum,
3350 S. George
Washington Boulevard,
Wichita 67210

CONTACTS
316.683.9242;
kansasaviation
museum.org;
www.wingsover
kansas.com

HOURS
Monday-Saturday
10 a.m.-5 p.m.;
Sunday 12-5 p.m.

Since 1920 Wichita aircraft companies have produced approximately a quarter million aircraft—more than any other city on earth. Wichita-built aircraft have included biplanes, sport planes, gliders, crop dusters, helicopters, amphibious aircraft, training planes, personal aircraft, and business jets. Wichita also has built hundreds of piston-engine and turboprop airliners, jet fighter-bombers, spy planes, and most of America's largest bombers—including every B-52 still flying.

WINTER LIVESTOCK, Dodge City

8 WONDER FINALIST: *Winter Livestock is a finalist for the 8 Wonders of Kansas Commerce because it is America's largest independent cattle auction company and one of the nation's oldest.*

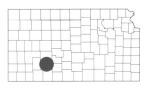

A native of Finney County, Kansas, and son of a rancher/homesteader, Karl Winter moved to Dodge City in 1936. There he purchased the town's livestock auction facilities and gradually built them into one of the nation's most successful livestock auction markets.

The Winter family's dedication to the cattle business has made the company industry leaders. Since 1936 Winter Livestock customers have sold more than 26 million cattle through its facilities, for a total cattle value of over $8 billion.

LOCATION
1414 E. Trail,
Dodge City 67801

CONTACTS
620.225.4159;
www.winterlivestock.com

HOURS
Wednesday (auction day)
10 a.m.-4 p.m.; sale barn
cafe open Monday-Friday
7 a.m.-2 p.m.

WOLF CREEK GENERATING STATION, Burlington

8 WONDER FINALIST: *Wolf Creek Generating Station is a finalist for the 8 Wonders of Kansas Commerce because it is the first and only nuclear power generating station in Kansas.*

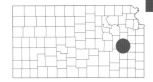

Wolf Creek has been safely providing clean energy to the citizens of Kansas and Missouri since 1985. The plant generates about 1,200 megawatts of electricity, which is enough for approximately 800,000 homes. Wolf Creek meets a growing energy demand and, because it uses nuclear technology instead of gas, oil, or coal as a heat source, it does not pollute the air or produce greenhouse gases. The plant contributes $165 million yearly to the local and state economy in the form of payroll, purchases, and taxes.

The Wolf Creek Environmental Education area is one mile east of U.S. 75 on 17th Road.

LOCATION
Dwight Eisenhower
Learning Center,
1550 Oxen Lane NE,
Burlington 66839.
From U.S. 75, 1 mile on
17th Road, then ¼ mile
south on Milo.

CONTACTS
620.364.8831,
ext. 4070;
jehagem@wcnoc.com;
www.wcnoc.com

HOURS
Presentations by
appointment.

Cuisine Top 8 Wonders

Bobo's Drive In, Topeka

Brookville Hotel, Abilene

Cozy Inn, Salina

Crawford County Fried Chicken, Crawford County

Free State Brewing Company, Lawrence

Guy and Mae's Tavern, Williamsburg

Hays House 1857 Historic Restaurant and Tavern, Council Grove

WheatFields Bakery Cafe, Lawrence

Cuisine Finalist Wonders

Anchor Inn, Hutchinson

C.W. Porubsky's Deli and Tavern, Topeka

Carolyn's Essenhaus, Arlington

Charlie's Mexican Restaurant, Leoti

Crazy R's, Goodland

Fritz's Union Station, Kansas City

Grand Central Hotel, Cottonwood Falls

Hibachi Hut, Manhattan

Homer's Drive Inn, Leavenworth

Josie's Ristorante, Scammon

NuWay Cafe, Wichita

Olive Tree Bistro, Wichita

Paolucci's Restaurant, Atchison

Pho Hoa 1 Restaurant, Garden City

Prairie Nut Hut, Altoona

Trapper's Bar and Grill, Simpson

Dave Kendall, video producer and host of *Sunflower Journeys*

Migrating to Kansas Territory from Kentucky, my great, great grandfather arrived in Council Grove the same year the Hays House opened for business: 1857. What do you suppose he saw on the menu? Would it have been anything like the current specialties: Grandma's Beef Brisket, Skillet-Fried Chicken, Beulah's Ham?

Thinking about my own dining experiences, I recall my earliest encounter with a menu. It happened at a restaurant called Mom's, where farmers and ranchers rubbed shoulders with railroaders and townsfolk. Nothing too fancy on the menu— just what you'd expect in a hometown cafe— but there was always a warm, friendly greeting and a full, satisfied belly afterwards.

Mom's closed long ago, but the Hays House isn't far down the road, nor is the Brookville Hotel. They've adapted to changing times and continue to attract appreciative patrons. I've heard stories from many folks who relish memorable experiences at Chicken Annie's or Chicken Mary's, Guy and Mae's, the Cozy Inn, or Bobo's. In more recent years we've seen newer establishments construct a connection to our heartland heritage— places such as Free State Brewery and Wheatfields in Lawrence. There are a lot more out there— new and old.

Eat well and enjoy!

Cuisine

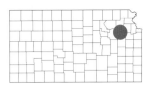

BOBO'S DRIVE IN, Topeka

TOP 8 WONDER: *Bobo's Drive In is one of the 8 Wonders of Kansas Cuisine because it is a throwback diner with carhop service, and its hamburgers, homemade onion rings, and apple pie have been long loved by hundreds of die-hard fans.*

LOCATION
2300 SW 10th,
Topeka 66604

CONTACTS
785.234.4511;
bobodrivein@yahoo.com

HOURS
Monday-Saturday
11 a.m.-8 p.m.

In 1953 Bob Bobo opened this diner at 10th and MacVicar and began cooking his mom and aunt's recipes. Several owners later, Richard and Tricia Marsh are continuing with these same recipes and keeping the loyalists happy.

The hamburgers are famous for the fresh but thin patties with salt, crisp edges, a slab of melting cheese, lettuce, and tomato. People love the hand-dipped onion rings and the homemade apple pie, which is made with a just-thick-enough crust and the smoothest, sweet cinnamon-covered tender apples; add a dollop of Satin-Freeze ice cream for a heavenly taste. As you might expect, the shakes are a popular item too.

Inside Bobo's you'll find a horseshoe counter with stools, plus a few booths for additional seating. It's a snug little place. But if you prefer car service, just park in a stall and a carhop will be out to take your order.

Cuisine

explorer extras...

A source of Topeka pride since 1899, beautiful Gage Park is just west of Gage Boulevard. It is home to the 1930 Reinisch Rose Garden, the Von Rohr Victorian Gardens, a mile-long mini-train, an operating 1908 carousel, and a zoo. Park entrances off 6th and 10th Avenues; 785.368.2449; www.topeka.org; hours and admission charges vary for each attraction. **ee**

BROOKVILLE HOTEL, Abilene

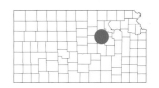

TOP 8 WONDER: *Brookville Hotel is one of the 8 Wonders of Kansas Cuisine because of its famous family-style chicken dinners that have been pleasing crowds since 1915. Originally located in the small town of Brookville, the restaurant was inside the town's historic hotel.*

Relishes, sweet-sour slaw, skillet-fried chicken, mashed potatoes and cream gravy, cream-style corn, baking powder biscuits with creamy butter and preserves, and home-style ice cream— that's the famous Brookville Hotel menu.

Helen Martin, daughter of original owners Gus and Mae Magnuson, first created the famous family-style chicken dinner in 1915. In 1982 the fourth-generation, Mark and Connie Martin, continued the tradition as the new owners. In 1999 they made the decision to move the restaurant from Brookville to Abilene. Although it was hard for many to see the historic restaurant leave Brookville, the Martins replicated the facade of the old hotel and retained its ambience. They have added colorful Kansas murals and still serve the famous menu on Blue Willow plates.

explorer extras...

Plan an evening in Abilene that includes the Great Plains Theatre. Set in an 1881 Victorian Romanesque limestone church, it has presented quality live professional performances since 1995. 300 N. Mulberry; 888.222.4574; www.greatplainstheatre.com. **ee**

LOCATION
105 E. Lafayette,
Abilene 67410

CONTACTS
785.263.2244;
cdmartin@
brookvillehotel.com;
www.brookvillehotel.com

HOURS
Wednesday-Friday
5-7:30 p.m.; Saturday
11:30 a.m.-2 p.m. and
4:30-7:30 p.m.; Sunday
11:30 a.m.-2 p.m. and
5-7 p.m. Reservations
recommended.

For more information, see page 46.

Cuisine

COZY INN, Salina

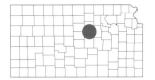

TOP 8 WONDER: *The Cozy Inn is one of the 8 Wonders of Kansas Cuisine because of its legendary sliders (buy 'em by the sack), its tiny hole-in-the-wall structure, and six-stool counter, all dating back to 1922.*

LOCATION
108 N. 7th,
Salina 67401

CONTACTS
785.825.2699;
steveh@cozyburger.com;
www.cozyburger.com

HOURS
Monday-Saturday
10 a.m.-9 p.m.;
Sunday 11 a.m.-8 p.m.

Cuisine

The Cozy's menu: Cozy Burger 85 cents or 24 for $18, chips, and soda. That's it!

The Cozy Inn opened in the spring of 1922 and three months later was sold to Robert Kinkel. After Kinkel's death, his wife, Kathryn, and her second husband, Dick Pickering, continued the Cozy legacy until their deaths in the 1990s.

Palm-sized hamburgers were grilled with a generous heap of onions. The burger became known as a "slider," likely because of the fry cooks' practice of sliding it down the counter on a sheet of waxed paper. The slider was dressed with pickle, catsup, and mustard . . . never cheese.

When the depression years hit America in the 1930s, joints like the Cozy Inn gained success by providing customers with a satisfying, yet inexpensive, meal. Kinkel kept the price of the Cozy burger at five cents for 20 years.

Steve Howard bought the Cozy Inn in 2007. Today you'll see him behind the counter flipping the mini-sized burgers and sliding them down the counter, just as it was done nearly 90 years ago.

explorer extras...

Immediately after the bombing of Pearl Harbor, news came that two military installations would be built in Saline County. In the next several years tens of thousands of young soldiers were assigned to Salina. The Cozy Inn gained great popularity during the war years as a hang-out for GIs needing a good meal on a soldier's pay.

ee

CRAWFORD COUNTY FRIED CHICKEN RESTAURANTS, Crawford County

TOP 8 WONDER: *Crawford County Fried Chicken Restaurants, as a group, are one of the 8 Wonders of Kansas Cuisine because these six individually owned restaurants have made Crawford County legendary for fried chicken since the 1930s.*

In chronological order:

CHICKEN ANNIE'S ORIGINAL, PITTSBURG

When Charlie Pichler was severely injured in a mining accident in 1933, his wife, Annie, became the family breadwinner. She started serving chicken dinners that consisted of three pieces of chicken, German potato salad, Cole slaw, a strip of pickled pepper, a slice of tomato, and bread, all for 75 cents. What began in 1934 continues today with Annie's children and grandchildren.

LOCATION 1143 E. 600th, Pittsburg 66762
CONTACTS 620.231.9460;
www.ckt.net/zagspage/cag/history.htm
HOURS Tuesday-Friday 4-8:30 p.m.; Saturday 4-9 p.m.;
Sunday 11 a.m.-8 p.m.

CHICKEN MARY'S, PITTSBURG

Joe Zerngast, a German immigrant, began working in the Pittsburg coal mines at the turn of the century, but due to poor health, he couldn't continue this job. To help support the family, his wife, Mary, turned to what she knew best, cooking. Soon she was serving customers fried chicken, German potato salad, and Cole slaw in their home. Starting in the early 1940s, Chicken Mary's is still going strong today.

LOCATION 1133 E. 600th, Pittsburg 66762
CONTACTS 620.231.9510
HOURS Tuesday-Friday 4-8:30 p.m.; Saturday 4-9 p.m.;
Sunday 11 a.m.-8 p.m.

GEBHARDT'S CHICKEN AND DINNERS, MULBERRY

Receiving his honorable discharge from the U.S. Army in 1942, Ted Gebhardt married Maycle Gilyeat and the couple moved to Ted's hometown of Mulberry. They purchased The Little Honky Tonk and operated it as a bar until 1946 when they converted it into a restaurant. Maycle, with her sister and grandmother, began experimenting with recipes and created a menu that featured fried chicken. Maycle's daughter, Meg Gebhardt, now runs the business.

LOCATION 124 N. 260th, Mulberry 66756
CONTACTS 620.764.3451; 620.249.9575;
gebhardtschicken@gmail.com
HOURS Friday-Saturday 4-9 p.m.;
Sunday 11 a.m.-7 p.m.; Monday 4-8 p.m.

BARTO'S IDLE HOUR, FRONTENAC

Ray Barto opened Barto's Idle Hour in the early 1950s and began pulling in customers by featuring polka dancing every Friday and Saturday night. Barto's, located in a residential area, serves its own special fried chicken recipe as well as delicious steaks. The Friday and Saturday night polka tradition continues.

LOCATION 210 S. Santa Fe, Frontenac 66763
CONTACTS 620.232.9834
HOURS Tuesday-Saturday 4-10 p.m.

PICHLER'S CHICKEN ANNIE'S, PITTSBURG

Two fried chicken families joined together when Anthony Pichler, grandson of the original Chicken Annie, married Donna Zerngast, granddaughter of the original Chicken Mary. With tasty fried chicken ingrained in both families, Anthony and Donna opened their own restaurant south of Pittsburg in 1970.

LOCATION 1271 S. 220th, Pittsburg 66762
CONTACTS 620.232.9260
HOURS Tuesday-Friday 4-8:30 p.m.; Saturday 4-9 p.m.;
Sunday 11 a.m.-8 p.m.

CHICKEN ANNIE'S OF GIRARD

Louis and Louella Lipoglav purchased the old Sunflower Tavern and Chicken Dinners restaurant near Girard in 1971. Louella, daughter of the original Chicken Annie, and her husband opened their new business as Chicken Annie's of Girard. The chicken here is cooked to order.

LOCATION 498 E. K-47, Girard 66743
CONTACTS 620.724.4090; razagone@ckt.net
HOURS Wednesday-Thursday 4-8:30 p.m.;
Friday-Saturday 4-9 p.m.; Sunday 11 a.m.-8 p.m.

Cuisine

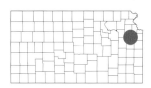

FREE STATE BREWING COMPANY, Lawrence

TOP 8 WONDER: *Free State Brewing Company is one of the 8 Wonders of Kansas Cuisine because, when it opened in 1989, it was the first legal brewery in Kansas since 1880. Along with its beer, Free State serves a variety of popular meals.*

LOCATION
630 Massachusetts,
Lawrence 66044

CONTACTS
785.843.4555;
fsb@freestatebrewing.com;
www.freestatebrewing.com

HOURS
Monday-Saturday
11 a.m.-midnight;
Sunday 12-11 p.m.

Cuisine

The vigorous debates prior to statehood about Kansas entering the Union as a slave or free state led to the name of this popular Lawrence restaurant.

Limestone walls, natural wood, and a two-story glass front give this college-town favorite a historic but casual feel.

Popular menu items include Chicken and Crawfish Gumbo (filled with spicy Andouille sausage, Cajun crawfish tails, stewed chicken, and a dark brown roux) and Blackbean Quesadillas featuring Alma cheese.

Free State's original and award-winning beers feature Wheat State Golden, Ad Astra Ale, Stormwatch Ale, Oatmeal Stout, and Dubbel Trouble Belgian.

explorer extras...

How does the term "free state" connect with the rich history of Lawrence? At the Lawrence Visitor Information Center (in a restored 1889 Union Pacific depot), find out about area attractions associated with the free-state controversy that led to the Civil War. N. 2nd and Locust; 785.865.4499; www.visitlawrence.com; Monday-Saturday 9 a.m.-5 p.m.; Sunday 1-5 p.m. **ee**

GUY AND MAE'S TAVERN, Williamsburg

TOP 8 WONDER: *Guy and Mae's Tavern, a family business since 1973, is one of the 8 Wonders of Kansas Cuisine because of its famous tender ribs served in foil and newspapers.*

Guy and Mae Kesner were the original owners of this hometown bar that brings hundreds of customers from I-35 and surrounding towns into tiny Williamsburg. Guy perfected his technique for barbecuing by testing the ribs on his trucker buddies when they stopped to visit. Mae invented the sauce.

For years now everyone has known about Guy and Mae's, and it's so popular you sometimes have to wait in line at the door. Inside the very ordinary-appearing tavern, booths are few, and customers often have to squeeze in at long picnic tables. In addition to the famous ribs, eager diners can enjoy beef, ham, turkey, and polish sausage barbequed sandwiches.

After Guy and Mae retired, their daughters Diana and Judy took over the business and have kept it going, with help from the grandchildren.

explorer extras...

About six miles north of Guy and Mae's, Pome on the Range Orchard and Winery operates a year-round marketplace offering fresh produce, fruit wines, and more. 2050 Idaho Road; 6 miles southwest of Ottawa at I-35 exit 176; 785.746.5492; www.pomeontherange.com; Monday-Saturday 10 a.m.-5 p.m.; Sunday 12-5 p.m. **ee**

GUY & MAE'S TAVERN
HOURS
TUES-SAT
11 AM - MIDNIGHT
CLOSED SUN & MON

LOCATION
119 W. William, Williamsburg 66095

CONTACTS
785.746.8830; judygm1@yahoo.com

HOURS
Tuesday-Saturday 11 a.m.-11 p.m.; closed last week of July through first week of August.

HAYS HOUSE 1857 RESTAURANT AND TAVERN,
Council Grove

TOP 8 WONDER: *Hays House 1857 Restaurant and Tavern is one of the 8 Wonders of Kansas Cuisine because it is the oldest continuously operating restaurant west of the Mississippi River.*

LOCATION
112 W. Main,
Council Grove 66846

CONTACTS
620.767.5911;
www.hayshouse1857.com

HOURS
Sunday-Thursday
6 a.m.-8 p.m.;
Friday-Saturday
6 a.m.-10 p.m.;
Reservations
recommended.

Cuisine

Seth Hays, founder of Council Grove and a great-grandson of Daniel Boone, built a log store on this site in 1847, and a decade later built the structure that partially remains today. Located on the Santa Fe Trail, it was a gathering place for meals but had many other purposes including a mail stop and a district court.

Today this National Historic Landmark serves steak, chicken fried steak, fried chicken, brisket, Beulah's ham, pasta, seafood dishes, and many salads, the Crunchy Chicken salad being a favorite. Choose the homemade Hays House Dill or Blue Cheese dressing for your salad. Other specialties include the famous fresh strawberry and peach pies and homemade ice cream.

explorer extras...
Seth Hays lived with his adopted daughter and his servant in an 1867 brick home, which today is operated as a museum. Wood and Hall Streets, Council Grove. A tall white marker stands at Hays' grave in Greenwood Cemetery, W. Main, Council Grove. His servant, Sally Taylor, is buried beside him, a topic of controversy at the time. To find the graves, from the cemetery office, go east to the next crossroads. **ee**

WHEATFIELDS BAKERY CAFE, Lawrence

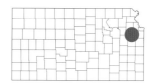

TOP 8 WONDER: *WheatFields Bakery Cafe is one of the 8 Wonders of Kansas Cuisine because it is a nationally ranked artisan bakery and serves healthy meals, featuring baked goods.*

The heart of WheatFields is its wood-fired oven, a room-sized brick silo that anchors the southwest corner of this cheery, open bakery cafe.

The 25-ton oven was brought in from Barcelona, Spain. Its rotating hearthstone (12 feet in diameter) is turned by a steering-wheel apparatus. It can bake about 200 loaves of bread at a time.

Bread varieties include Ciabatta, Country French, Kalamata Olive, Pecan Raisin, Rustic Italian Round, Semolina, and Spelt.

Serving breakfast, sandwiches, soups, salads, and appetizers, in addition to loaves of artisan bread and other pastries, this bakery has been keeping customers happy since 1995.

explorer extras...

A standout attraction in Lawrence, the Robert J. Dole Institute of Politics on the KU West Campus is an impressively designed facility featuring state-of-the-art visual and audio displays about the senator's achievements as a KU student, a World War II soldier, and a politician. 2350 Petefish; 785.864.4900; www.doleinstitute.org; Monday-Saturday 9 a.m.-5 p.m.; Sunday 12-5 p.m. **ee**

LOCATION
904 Vermont,
Lawrence 66044

CONTACTS
785.841.5553;
wfbc@wheatfieldsbakery.com;
www.wheatfieldsbakery.com

HOURS
Monday-Friday
6:30 a.m.-8 p.m.
(breakfast served until
11 a.m.); Saturday
6:30 a.m.-6:30 p.m.;
Sunday 7:30 a.m.-4 p.m.
(breakfast served until
1 p.m. on weekends).

Cuisine

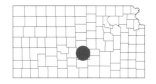

ANCHOR INN, Hutchinson

8 WONDER FINALIST: *The Anchor Inn is a finalist for the 8 Wonders of Kansas Cuisine because the dedication of the Flores family has made this Mexican restaurant a local institution.*

The Anchor Inn was started at 126 S. Main by Antonio and Rachel Flores in 1977 and eventually expanded into two adjoining buildings. Fourth-generation family members now work at the restaurant, which is the place to bump into friends and have family reunions. Many regulars come for their Anchor "fix" and their favorites, such as the tostados, fajitas, the red beer, and especially the flour tacos.

C.W. PORUBSKY'S DELI AND TAVERN, Topeka

8 WONDER FINALIST: *C.W. Porubsky's Deli and Tavern is a finalist for the 8 Wonders of Kansas Cuisine because its chili, hot pickles, and cold cuts have made the tavern a 60-year fixture in Topeka's "Little Russia."*

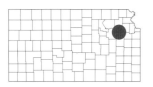

Descendants of the Volga Germans who settled here at the turn of the 20th century, Charlie and Lydia Porubsky opened the grocery store and tavern in 1947. Connected by a doorway, the west half of the unassuming building is a small grocery store, and the east half is the deli/tavern. Politicians, business leaders, and laborers all make the trip across the tracks hoping to find an open seat (occupancy 36), especially at the start of chili season (September 1).

CAROLYN'S ESSENHAUS, Arlington

8 WONDER FINALIST: *Carolyn's Essenhaus is a finalist for the 8 Wonders of Kansas Cuisine because this Amish Mennonite establishment has been using family and ethnic recipes for 20 years.*

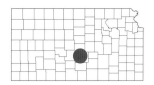

LOCATION
104 E. Main,
Arlington 67514

CONTACTS
620.538.4711;
www.carolynsessenhaus.
com

HOURS
Monday-Friday
6 a.m.-8:30 p.m.;
Saturday 6 a.m.-
2:30 p.m.; breakfast
served until 10:30 a.m.

Carolyn Bontrager's family descends from Switzerland and Germany, the origins of most of the recipes at this restaurant, which opened in 1989. Her father is at the cafe every weekday at 3:30 a.m. baking pies, and her mom makes the pie crusts.

Signature menu items include skillet-fried chicken, verenike, chicken-fried steak, lemon meringue pie, and the pastry bar's cinnamon rolls and bienenstich, a coffee cake.

CHARLIE'S MEXICAN RESTAURANT, Leoti

8 WONDER FINALIST: *Charlie's Mexican Restaurant is a finalist for the 8 Wonders of Kansas Cuisine because it is one of the first Mexican restaurants established in western Kansas and it continues to use family recipes.*

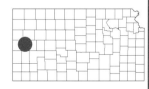

Cuisine

LOCATION
510 E. Broadway,
Leoti 67861

CONTACTS
620.375.4541

HOURS
Monday-Saturday
5-9 p.m.

Coming to Kansas from Mexico when he was five years old, Charlie Campas always dreamed of opening a restaurant, which he did in 1962. Campas is gone now but son Gary and his wife, Sheila, continue the tradition. Everything is homemade, and menu favorites include Charlie's Special (fried flour tortilla with refried beans and Charlie's pork chili topped with cheese, lettuce, and tomato), chile rellenos, barbacoa, and chicken avocado salad.

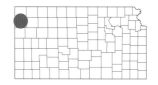

CRAZY R'S BAR & GRILL, Goodland

8 WONDER FINALIST: *Crazy R's Bar & Grill is a finalist for the 8 Wonders of Kansas Cuisine because of its excellent food, fun, decor, and service, and the personality of owner Rod Cooper.*

LOCATION
1618 Main,
Goodland 67735

CONTACTS
785.890.3430

HOURS
Monday-Saturday
11 a.m.-9 p.m.
(Mountain Time)

Inside a plain metal building, Crazy R's walls and corners are filled with Cooper's antique-collecting results. Since 1987 dining has been an enjoyable event at this bar and grill.

Cooper does all the cooking from recipes he stores in his head. He also uses fresh meat purchased from the local meat locker. Prime rib night is Wednesday and steaks are served 5-9 p.m. Other favorites include hand-breaded pork tenderloins, Crazy R burgers, Rajin' Cajun burgers, and Papa's chicken-fried bacon.

FRITZ'S UNION STATION, Kansas City

8 WONDER FINALIST: *Fritz's Union Station is a finalist for the 8 Wonders of Kansas Cuisine because it dates to 1954 and is beloved for its food delivery system— a miniature railroad.*

This neighborhood diner features miniature railroad cars to help the waitresses serve customers. The cars circle the restaurant on an overhead track, stop at your table, and lower your order on a miniature elevator.

Fritz's most famous burger, the Gen-Dare, comes with crunchy hash browns, grilled onions, and melted cheese. The thick meaty chili and handmade shakes also are local favorites.

LOCATION
250 N. 18th,
Kansas City 66102

CONTACTS
913.281.2777

HOURS
Monday 6 a.m.-3 p.m.;
Tuesday-Saturday
6 a.m.-8:30 p.m.

GRAND CENTRAL HOTEL, Cottonwood Falls

8 WONDER FINALIST: *The Grand Central Hotel is a finalist for the 8 Wonders of Kansas Cuisine because it is the state's only AAA Four Diamond Historic Country Inn/Restaurant, and customers attest that its steaks are the best in Kansas.*

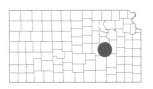

LOCATION
215 Broadway,
Cottonwood Falls 66845

CONTACTS
620.273.6763;
suzan.barnes@
sbcglobal.net;
www.grandcentral
hotel.com

HOURS
Monday-Saturday
11 a.m.-4 p.m. (lunch);
5-9 p.m. (dinner).
Reservations
recommended.

The hotel, built in 1884 and remodeled in 1995, features original brick walls and stockyard brick flooring. An outdoor courtyard allows you to enjoy the Flint Hills town atmosphere. Proprietor Suzan Barnes says this is where Old West charm meets New World hospitality.

The Sterling Silver prime rib, with its reputation as Kansas's best, is featured on Saturdays.

HIBACHI HUT, Manhattan

8 WONDER FINALIST: *The Hibachi Hut is a finalist for the 8 Wonders of Kansas Cuisine because it has been a mainstay in Aggieville since 1959 and is famous for Cajun/Creole recipes and American specialties.*

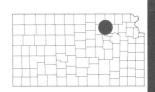

LOCATION
608 N. 12th,
Manhattan 66502

CONTACTS
785.539.9393;
thehut1959@yahoo.com;
www.hibachihut.com

HOURS
Monday, Wednesday,
Thursday-Saturday
11 a.m.-9 p.m.;
Sunday 10 a.m.-8:30 p.m.

When the Hibachi Hut opened, food was cooked on a hibachi grill (a small grill). A 40-year-old painting of a hibachi grill is still on "the Hut's" front window.

Some of the Hibachi Hut's most popular items include crawfish etouffee with blackened catfish, the Belly Bomb hamburger, gumbo, red beans and rice, and homemade bread pudding with whiskey sauce.

Cuisine

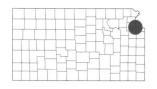

HOMER'S DRIVE INN, Leavenworth

8 WONDER FINALIST: *Homer's Drive Inn is a finalist for the 8 Wonders of Kansas Cuisine because since 1931 it has been a classic drive-in (with carhops) and offers full-menu breakfast, lunch, dinner, and fountain service.*

LOCATION
1320 S. 4th,
Leavenworth 66048

CONTACTS
913.651.3500

HOURS
Monday-Saturday
6 a.m.-8 p.m. (breakfast
until 10:30 a.m.); Sunday
6:30 a.m.-8 p.m.
(breakfast until 11 a.m.)

Homer McKelvey began the tradition of serving nickel mugs of root beer from a wooden stand. In those early days McKelvey's waiters dressed in long-sleeved shirts and ties to offer carhop service and dispense hot dogs, hamburgers, and root beer to customers driving Model Ts.

Longtime servers Anna Brown and Marla Bockman continue to feature fresh hamburgers, soda fountain favorites, and daily specials. Carhop service remains.

JOSIE'S RISTORANTE, Scammon

8 WONDER FINALIST: *Josie's Ristorante is a finalist for the 8 Wonders of Kansas Cuisine because of its reputation for excellent Italian food made from recipes that Grandmother Josie brought from Italy in 1904.*

LOCATION
400 N. Main,
Scammon 66773

CONTACTS
620.479.8202

HOURS
Wednesday-Saturday
4-9 p.m.

Frank and Josie Saporito came to this county to take advantage of the mining jobs in Cherokee and Crawford Counties. In 1986 the Saporitos' grandson Mike and his wife, Sally, converted a vacant 1890s grocery store into a restaurant in the old mining town of Scammon. Using Josie's old-world recipes, Sally makes her signature sauce and dough fresh each morning for all the pasta including lasagna, ravioli, and spaghetti.

NUWAY CAFE, Wichita

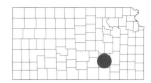

8 WONDER FINALIST: *The NuWay Cafe is a finalist for the 8 Wonders of Kansas Cuisine because it dates to 1930 and is famous for its crumbled beef sandwiches.*

The NuWay tradition began on July 4, 1930, at its present location on West Douglas in a former Phillips 66 station. Today NuWay sandwiches are still made with the same recipe, and customers still sit on stools at the Formica counter. The crumbled ground beef delight is served on a standard hamburger bun and is topped with pickles, diced onions, and mustard.

Other favorites are the creamy homemade root beer served in a frosty mug and the famous homemade crispy onion rings.

LOCATION
1416 W. Douglas,
Wichita 67203

CONTACTS
316.267.1131;
www.nuwaycafe.com

HOURS
Daily 10:30 a.m.-9 p.m.

Cuisine

OLIVE TREE BISTRO, Wichita

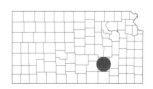

8 WONDER FINALIST: *Olive Tree Bistro was a finalist for the 8 Wonders of Kansas Cuisine because it was the flagship of the Latour fine-dining restaurants, and because of its award-winning Mediterranean cuisine and service.*

Named a finalist for the contest in 2009, this fine restaurant closed in 2010.

PAOLUCCI'S RESTAURANT, Atchison

8 WONDER FINALIST: *Paolucci's Restaurant is a finalist for the 8 Wonders of Kansas Cuisine because it has been serving Italian recipes since 1983 that came to America with Grandma Paolucci in 1894.*

LOCATION
113 S. 3rd,
Atchison 66002

CONTACTS
913.367.6105;
www.paoluccibegley.com

HOURS
Monday-Saturday
6 a.m.-9 p.m.;
Sunday 7 a.m.-1 p.m.

Coming from Frosolone, Italy, Rosa (Grandma) Paolucci, her husband, Dominic, and his brother Felix opened a fruit market in downtown Atchison. In 1983 Paolucci descendant Mike Begley and wife, Margie, started their restaurant and deli in the same building. A grandson's involvement makes Paolucci's a fifth-generation family business.

Specials include Italian dinners featuring made-from-scratch spaghetti sauce and the Guiseppe Burger, a fresh patty, seasoned with the secret Paolucci sauce.

PHO HOA 1 VIETNAMESE RESTAURANT, Garden City

8 WONDER FINALIST: *Pho Hoa 1 is a finalist for the 8 Wonders of Kansas Cuisine because it is the most renowned Vietnamese restaurant in the state and uses fresh ingredients from the local Asian market.*

LOCATION
713 E. Fulton,
Garden City 67846

CONTACTS
620.276.3393

HOURS
Monday-Saturday
(closed Wednesday)
10 a.m.-2:30 p.m.
and 4:30-8:30 p.m.;
Sunday 10 a.m.-3 p.m.

Khanh and Ha Nguyen fled from South Vietnam in 1979 and for a year lived in a refugee camp in Malaysia. When granted the right to come to the United States, they moved to Houston and then to Garden City in 1987 to open a restaurant. The Nguyens almost gave up before people of every culture began to appreciate their delicious Vietnamese food. Today son Dat works with his parents, making the popular local restaurant a second-generation family business.

PRAIRIE NUT HUT, Altoona

8 WONDER FINALIST: *The Prairie Nut Hut is a finalist for the 8 Wonders of Kansas Cuisine because of its widespread reputation since the 1960s as a colorful cafe serving mountain oysters.*

The Prairie Nut Hut's white wooden building is covered with signs indicating that even the owners have fun with the cafe's name. Opened as a tavern in the 1940s, it started featuring mountain oysters (calf fries) around the late 1960s. Today it still offers its namesake along with many other choices including fresh, juicy hamburgers and hand-battered chicken-fried steaks.

You can throw peanuts on the floor, but you can't squeeze more than 40 people into the tiny Nut Hut.

LOCATION
1306 Quincy,
Altoona 66710

CONTACTS
620.568.2900

HOURS
Tuesday-Friday
4-9 p.m.;
Saturday 11 a.m.-8 p.m.

TRAPPER'S BAR AND GRILL, Simpson

8 WONDER FINALIST: *Trapper's Bar and Grill is a finalist for the 8 Wonders of Kansas Cuisine because its charcoal grilled steaks, chicken-fried steaks, and ribs bring more people to town than live there.*

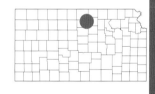

Tony and Becky Prochaska opened the cafe in 1994 with the desire to "stuff the customers like Tony's Grandma's cooking stuffed him." The name of the restaurant comes from Tony's pastime of trapping. The walls are decorated with old traps, hunting items, taxidermy displays, and old license plates.

Four rustic dining rooms have been added to increase the capacity to 160. Often every chair is full, especially on Tuesday's dollar hamburger night.

LOCATION
304 S. Elkhorn,
Simpson 67478

CONTACTS
785.593.6678

HOURS
Tuesday-Saturday
8 a.m.-10 p.m.

Customs Top 8 Wonders

Bringing musicians together, Cottonwood Falls

Chanting a school fight song, Lawrence

Clicking your heels three times…, Liberal and Wamego

Commemorating Veterans Day, Emporia

Displaying an ethnic handicraft, Lindsborg

Ordering a soda fountain treat, statewide

Riding a carousel, Abilene and Leavenworth

Using post rock for fencing, Smoky Hills region and LaCrosse

Customs Finalist Wonders

Attending a community dinner theater, Topeka

Building wide main streets, Plains

Checking on the weather, Harper

Connecting underground businesses, Ellinwood

Converting rails to trails, Ottawa to Iola

Cruising main street, Blue Rapids

Putting shoes on a tree, Wetmore

Racing greyhounds, Abilene

Racing motorcycles, Marquette

Racing on a dirt track, Belleville

Reciting and chanting the Psalms, Atchison

Recognizing those who came in second, Norton

Saving a seat, Concordia

Saving twine, Cawker City

Swimming in the summer, Garden City

Walking to school, Franklin and Arma

By Martha Slater Farrell, owner of First Generation Video

Customs is perhaps the most elusive of the 8 Wonders because they are hidden in our daily routines. My favorite memories of a happy childhood in Hutchinson include spending hot summer afternoons lolling at the swimming pool, evenings "dragging Main" (our wide main street), and sucking on a chocolate malt at the old-fashioned soda fountain. Life was good, and these were the customs that made it good in my hometown. When I saw the 24 finalists for Kansas customs, it made me smile to realize how many thousands of people feel as I do.

As we get older we revel in finding customs new to us— like chanting our university's fight song at a big game, or listening to homespun music as we relax in lawn chairs smack dab in the middle of the street. Lindsborg enchants us with its Swedish customs, and Cawker City amuses with the quirkiness of a local farmer.

Customs abound in our hobbies, daily habits, rituals, and obsessions. They can embarrass us (for example, when people halfway across the world click their heels when they learn we're from Kansas). But most of all, customs are the simple moments that cause us to treasure life in Kansas and remind us "There's no place like home." We celebrate them here.

Customs

BRINGING MUSICIANS TOGETHER, Cottonwood Falls

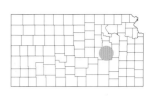

TOP 8 WONDER: *Bringing musicians together, as happens every Friday night in Cottonwood Falls, is one of the 8 Wonders of Kansas Customs.*

Every Friday night since October 1999, Sue Smith has welcomed people to the Emma Chase Cafe in beautiful downtown Cottonwood Falls. If weather permits, the public sets up lawn chairs on the main street and listens as musicians play. Cold weather sends everyone indoors—to the cafe or the Emma Chase Music Hall inside a PWA building.

People don't have to remember an intricate schedule—it's really every Friday at 7:30 p.m. Admission is free.

An evening count of musicians might be anywhere from four to thirty. First-time visitors are amazed at this unique phenomenon of regular people, with varying levels of musicianship, taking turns leading songs while other musicians play along.

Each Friday features a specific music category: acoustic country, bluegrass, gospel, old-time rock n' roll, and on the occasional fifth Friday, old-time music.

From 5:00 to 8:00 each Friday evening "The Emma" offers fried catfish dinners to enjoy before listening to great music. It's all part of the weekly fun!

explorer extras...
One of the greatest musical gatherings in the Midwest, the Walnut Valley Festival is held each September in Winfield. Performances are 9 a.m.-midnight on four stages for five days. 620.221.3250; www.wvfest.com. **ee**

LOCATION
317 Broadway,
Cottonwood Falls 66845

CONTACTS
620.273.6020;
prairiemaid@
sbcglobal.net;
www.emmachasecafe.com

HOURS
Every Friday
at 7:30 p.m.

Customs

CHANTING A SCHOOL FIGHT SONG, Lawrence

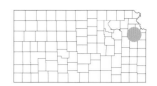

TOP 8 WONDER: *Chanting a school fight song, such as the "Rock Chalk Jayhawk" chant, is one of the 8 Wonders of Kansas Customs. The chant is heard most often at a University of Kansas basketball or football game.*

The chant words are etched in stone on the first floor of the Kansas Union, and a display next to the steps illustrates the cheer and its history. A panel documenting the Rock Chalk story is on the union's fourth floor.

KU's world-famous Rock Chalk chant evolved from a cheer that chemistry professor E.H.S. Bailey created for the KU science club in 1886. Bailey's version was "Rah, Rah, Jayhawk, KU," repeated three times. The "rahs" were later replaced by "Rock Chalk," a transposition of chalk rock, the name for the limestone outcropping on Mount Oread, the site of the KU campus.

The chant is heard at the beginning of each KU game, following the "alma mater" song. Fans begin the chant slowly and end in a burst of increased volume and speed. Additionally, near the end of a game, much to opponents' dismay, the haunting chant gradually emerges from the fans when a KU victory is imminent.

explorer extras...

Standing just south of the KU football stadium, the Memorial Campanile and Carillon is one of the most striking features on campus. It is a towering monument honoring the university's students, alumni, and personnel who died in or served during World War II. The carillon bells provide occasional music and strike on the quarter hour. Designed by Bernard "Poco" Frazier, the tall bronze doors at both entrances contain symbolic themes about the war and about early Kansas. Memorial Drive, Kansas University campus. **ee**

LOCATION
Kansas Union,
1301 Jayhawk Boulevard,
Lawrence 66046

CONTACTS
785.864.3256;
kurelations@ku.edu;
www.youtube.com/
watch?v=h51be27dN8c

HOURS
During the school year,
Monday-Saturday
7 a.m.-11 p.m.;
Sunday 12-9 p.m.

Customs

WELCOME TO
TRADITIONS N

CLICKING YOUR HEELS THREE TIMES…,
Liberal and Wamego

TOP 8 WONDER: *Clicking your heels three times and saying "There's no place like home," a famous phrase from the* Wizard of Oz, *is one of the 8 Wonders of Kansas Customs. Liberal and Wamego exhibit extensive Oz attractions.*

This custom has its roots in the 1900 L. Frank Baum book *The Wonderful Wizard of Oz* and in the 1939 MGM musical *The Wizard of Oz*, whose stories have strong and widely known Kansas connections.

WAMEGO

Home to one of the world's largest privately owned Oz collections, the OZ Museum is a bright, colorful stop on Wamego's main street.

Fans start their museum journey in the sepia-toned Auntie Em's Gift Shop, and then pass through the screen door into the Technicolor world of Oz.

The Yellow Brick Road continues past displays that feature L. Frank Baum, the Munchkins, Dorothy, Tin Man, Scarecrow, the Wicked Witch, Flying Monkey, Winkie Guard, Glinda the Good Witch, the Wizard, and the 1950s.

Also on exhibit is memorabilia from the MGM musical starring Judy Garland, earlier "Oz" silent films (one of which starred Oliver Hardy, of Laurel and Hardy fame, as the Tin Man), and the Broadway musical *Wicked*. The OZ Museum offers all things Oz, from the earliest Baum books to Parker Brothers board games and today's collectibles.

LOCATION
511 Lincoln, Wamego 66547

CONTACTS 785.458.8686; ozmuseum@wamego.net; www.ozmuseum.com

HOURS
Monday-Saturday 10 a.m.-5 p.m.; Sunday 12-5 p.m.; December to February, Monday-Saturday 10 a.m.-4 p.m.; Sunday 12-3 p.m. Admission charge.

explorer extras…

A well-known Wamego attraction, the Schonhoff Dutch Mill was built with native limestone in 1879 by Dutch immigrant John Schonhoff. In 1924 the 40-foot-tall mill was taken apart stone by stone and moved 12 miles to the city park site. E. 4th; 877.292.6346; www.visitwamego.com. **ee**

LIBERAL

A 1907 farmhouse was donated to the Seward County Historical Society in 1981 and moved to its present location on the Coronado Museum grounds. It has been carefully restored and furnished to replicate Dorothy's house as it appeared in the musical *The Wizard of Oz*. In the film, Dorothy's affection for her house and farmstead made her realize "There's no place like home."

Next to Dorothy's House, visitors may tour the *Land of Oz*, a 5,000-square-foot exhibit. The animated journey follows the Yellow Brick Road past good and bad witches, the Munchkins, talking trees, winged monkeys, and of course Dorothy, Scarecrow, Tin Man, the Cowardly Lion, and Toto, too.

Creator Linda Windler, assisted by her parents, Wilmer "Ed" and Lucile Edson, moved the Land of Oz to Liberal from Topeka in the spring of 1992. Much of the display was created using recycled materials and common household items, such as carpet tubes to re-create the Emerald City and discarded plastic flowers from various stores to make the Munchkinland gardens.

LOCATION 567 E. Cedar, Liberal 67901

CONTACTS 620.624.7624; 800.542.3725; tourism@cityofliberal.org; www.dorothyshouse.com

HOURS Labor Day to Memorial Day, Tuesday-Saturday 9 a.m.-5 p.m.; Sunday 1-5 p.m.; Memorial Day to Labor Day, Monday-Saturday 9 a.m.-6 p.m.; Sunday 1-6 p.m. Admission charge.

explorer extras…

Like the Land of Oz, pancakes are especially significant to Liberal. Honor the town's annual International Pancake Day Race with breakfast or lunch at the Pancake House. Or try the Kijafa crepe (sour cherries cooked in Kijafa wine). 640 E. Pancake; 620.624.8585; Tuesday-Sunday 6 a.m.-1 p.m. Learn more about the International Pancake Day Race at www.pancakeday.net. **ee**

Customs

TOP 8 WONDER: *Commemorating Veterans Day is one of the 8 Wonders of Kansas Customs. This national holiday is especially significant to Emporia, the Official Founding City of Veterans Day.*

Emporia holds this official title because an Emporia man is responsible for changing the name of this commemorative day in the United States from Armistice Day to Veterans Day.

Emporia shoe repairman Alvin J. "Al" King and his wife, Gertrude, helped raise a nephew, John E. Cooper, who later served in the U.S. Army. Cooper was killed in action in Germany on December 20, 1944. Grief over the young man's death started King searching for a way to honor not only his nephew but all veterans who fight in all wars and serve during peace.

King began his campaign to change an existing national holiday, Armistice Day, established to commemorate the armistice signed near the end of World War I, to Veterans Day. He gained support

from U.S. Representative Ed Rees of Emporia who agreed to take King's idea to Washington, D.C. The bill passed the House and Senate, and President Eisenhower signed the bill to establish Veterans Day as a national holiday.

The nation celebrated its first Veterans Day on November 11, 1954. On October 31, 2003, Congress declared Emporia the Official Founding City of Veterans Day.

A display at Lyon County Museum tells of the effort to create Veterans Day.

explorer extras...

All Veterans Memorial park, the first in the United States, features a World War II Sherman tank, a memorial to Emporian Sergeant Grant Timmerman, a Vietnam Veterans Memorial, the Purple Heart Monument, and the USS Emporia bell. Operation Enduring Freedom and Operation Iraqi Freedom, a monument to recognize the latest wars, was dedicated in November 2003. 933 S. Commercial, Emporia; 800.279.3730; visitors@ emporiakschamber.org. **ee**

LOCATION
Lyon County Museum, 118 E. 6th, Emporia 66801

CONTACTS
620.340.6310; visitors@ emporiakschamber.org; www.lyoncounty historicalsociety.org

HOURS
Tuesday-Saturday 1-5 p.m.

Customs

TOP 8 WONDER: *Displaying an ethnic handicraft, such as Swedish Dala horses, is one of the 8 Wonders of Kansas Customs. For many years this ethnic symbol has been designed, produced, and exhibited in Lindsborg.*

The Dala horse is a wooden tail-less, stubby horse whose origins date to early Swedish loggers and soldiers who whittled these horses for their children. The design derives its name from the Dalarna Province of Sweden, where the wooden horses, colorfully and decoratively painted, were popularized in the 1800s.

By the 1990s the traditional Dala horse symbol—orange in color and decorated with white flowing kurbits—had been adapted in hundreds of daily uses, large and small, in Lindsborg. In 2000 the community created the Wild Dala Horses, a pop-art twist to the traditional handicraft.

Twenty-nine of these fiberglass, pony-sized horses have been placed throughout the town. Decorated by local artists, each publicly displayed Wild Dala Horse has a distinctive and humorous play-on-words name, from Dalallama Telecomma to Hello Dala!, which honors the town's summer outdoor theater.

explorer extras...

Enjoy a traditional Swedish breakfast at Lindsborg's Swedish Country Inn. The public may join overnight guests for a buffet of Swedish meatballs, lingonberries, eggs, porridge, cheese, cold meats, pickled herring, waffles with lingonberry syrup, and rye bread. 112 W. Lincoln; 800.231.0266; www.swedishcountryinn.com; daily 7-10 a.m. **ee**

LOCATION
Throughout downtown Lindsborg 67456; maps of Wild Dala Horse locations are available at the Travel Information Center, 114 N. Main

CONTACTS
785.227.8687; cvbdir@lindsborgcity.org; www.lindsborgcity.org

Customs

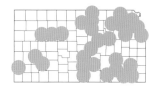

TOP 8 WONDER: *Ordering a treat from an old-fashioned soda fountain is one of the 8 Wonders of Kansas Customs. Thirty-eight operating soda fountains remain in Kansas.*

In the first half of the 20th century, most Kansas towns claimed at least one soda fountain. At the start of the 21st century, we had about 48. Now, in 2011, we are down to 38.

A few of the remaining soda fountains at their original locations date to the 1920s or earlier. Some contain original features such as a back bar, mirror, brass rail, and marble counter. Those built after 1950 have Formica counter tops, and some early marble tops have been converted to Formica.

Potwin Drug in Topeka boasts the oldest (1902) operating fountain in the state. Others represent the 1950s: Ball Brothers Drug in Atchison sports a loud red-and-white tile counter; Cardinal Drug in Chanute displays Coca Cola memorabilia throughout. Opened most recently are fountains in Quinter, Canton, and Bennington.

Purists love and want syrups and working spigots, but our soda fountain requirements are more lenient. Parts to equip or restore a traditional fountain are expensive and hard to find, and someone who can install them is rare.

Almost everyone loves the nostalgia of the old-fashioned fountain. The following is a list of all 38 in Kansas. Try to visit them all!

ABILENE, Bankes Drug, 304 N. Broadway. 785.263.4330. Monday-Friday 8:30 a.m.-6 p.m.; Saturday 8:30 a.m.-1 p.m. 1920s seven-stool fountain with round mirror and 1972 Formica counter.

AGENDA, Hope Floats, 400 block of Railroad Street. 785.732.6595. Wednesday-Saturday 10 a.m.-5 p.m. Five-stool fountain with marble counter, back bar, and mirror.

ANTHONY, Irwin Potter Drug, 202 W. Main. 620.842.5119. Monday-Saturday 8 a.m.-6 p.m. 1968 11-stool fountain with u-shaped bar and Formica counter.

ARKANSAS CITY, Graves Drug, 212 S. Summit. 620.442.8317. Monday-Friday 9 a.m.-6 p.m.; Saturday 9 a.m.-2:30 p.m. 10-stool fountain; lunch served.

ATCHISON, Ball Brothers Healthmart, 504 Commercial. 913.367.0332. Monday-Saturday 9 a.m.-7 p.m. 17-stool 1950s fountain and grill.

BELOIT, Perfect Pair, 100 S. Mill. 785.738.3000. Monday-Friday 9 a.m.-5:30 p.m.; Saturday 9 a.m.-3 p.m. Six-stool fountain with marble counter and 1901 back bar and mirror.

BENNINGTON, The Linger Longer, 119 N. Nelson. 785.820.6050. Monday-Friday 3-7 p.m.; Saturday 3-9 p.m. 1912 five-stool fountain with marble counter, back bar, and mirror; syrups are mixed using spigots.

CANEY, Gabby's Flea Market, 204 W. 4th. 620.870.9123. Saturday 10 a.m.-4 p.m.; Sunday 1-4 p.m. 1935 four-stool fountain with Formica counter.

CANTON, Soda n' Suds, 116 S. Main. 620.350.8006. Tuesday-Saturday 11 a.m.-8 p.m.; Sunday 4-8 p.m. 1939 seven-stool fountain; originally in Riley, Kansas.

CHANUTE, Cardinal Drug Store, 103 E. Main. 620.431.9150. Monday-Friday 9 a.m.-6 p.m.; Saturday 9 a.m.-2 p.m. 1937 Bastain-Blessing fountain with marble counter and a 1914 oak back bar with mirror and cabinets; guests sit at ice cream tables and chairs.

CHETOPA, Riggs Drug, 426 Maple. 620.236.7272. Monday-Friday 8:30 a.m.-5:30 p.m.; Saturday 8:30 a.m.-1 p.m. 1920s 10-stool fountain with back bar, mirror, and Formica counter.

CIMARRON, Clark Pharmacy, 101 S. Main. 620.855.2242. Monday-Friday 8:30 a.m.-6 p.m.; Saturday 9 a.m.-5 p.m. 1920s seven-stool fountain with tile counter and chrome spigots.

COUNCIL GROVE, Aldrich Apothecary, 115 W. Main. 620.767.6731. Monday-Friday 9 a.m.-5:30 p.m.; Saturday 9 a.m.-4 p.m. 1920s six-stool fountain with tile and marble counter and working chrome spigots.

Customs

171

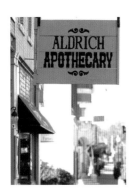

GARDEN CITY, Traditions Soda & Sandwich, 121 Grant, 620.275.1998. Monday-Friday 9 a.m.-6 p.m.; Saturday 9 a.m.-5 p.m. Seven-stool fountain with Formica counter; a 1950s sign states that three dips of ice cream were 24 cents.

GARDNER, Gardner Pharmacy, 131 E. Main. 913.856.8106. Monday-Friday 9 a.m.-6 p.m.; Saturday 9 a.m.-1 p.m. Five-stool fountain with marble counter, original freezer, spigots, syrup rail, and sinks; modern back bar with mirror.

GLASCO, Hodge Podge, 113 E. Main. 785.568.2542. Monday-Friday 9 a.m.-5 p.m.; Saturday 9 a.m.-12 p.m. 1932 six-stool fountain with back bar and mirror.

HAMILTON, Holmes Sundry, 101 E. Main. 620.678.3341. Monday-Friday 6 a.m.-6 p.m.; Saturday 6 a.m.-4 p.m.; Sunday 7 a.m.-2 p.m. 1920s six-stool fountain with marble base, original syrup pumps and spigots.

HAYS, Soda Shoppe, 800 Main, inside Northwestern Office Supply Store. 785.625.7323. Monday-Friday 11 a.m.-5 p.m.; Saturday 11 a.m.-4 p.m. 1950s seven-stool fountain with Formica counter; lunch served.

HERINGTON, Boelling Pharmacy, 2 W. Main. 785.258.3703. Monday-Friday 8 a.m.-6 p.m.; Saturday 8 a.m.-1 p.m. 1910-1915 six-stool fountain with back bar, mirror, and brass rail.

HOLTON, Koger Variety, 417 New York. 785.364.3321. Monday-Saturday 9 a.m.-5 p.m.; Sunday 12-4 p.m. 1920s five-stool fountain with original tile counter and mirror.

HOWARD, Batson's Drug, 102 N. Wabash. 620.374.2265. Monday-Friday 8 a.m.-6 p.m.; Saturday 8 a.m.-2 p.m. Eight-stool fountain with back bar, mirrors, and Formica counter; rebuilt in 1953.

HUTCHINSON, Fraese Drug, 100 N. Main. 620.662.4477. Monday-Friday 8:30 a.m.-2 p.m.; Saturday 8:30-10:30 a.m. 1939 12-stool fountain dates to the opening of Fraese Drug.

INDEPENDENCE, The American Soda Fountain and Sandwich Shoppe, 205 N. Penn. 620.331.0604. Monday-Friday 7:30 a.m.-6 p.m.; Saturday 9 a.m.-1 p.m. 1930s 15-stool fountain with renovated Formica counter; lunch served.

JOHNSON, The Old Store, 112 S. Main. 620.492.1478. Monday 10 a.m.-2 p.m.; Tuesday-Friday 10 a.m.-5:30 p.m.; Saturday 10 a.m.-4 p.m. 1950s four-stool Stanley Knight fountain with original 1920 oak back bar.

LEAVENWORTH, The Corner Pharmacy, 429 Delaware. 913.682.1602. Monday-Saturday 7:30 a.m.-5 p.m. 15-stool Victorian-era replica fountain with mahogany bar and faux marble counter.

MARQUETTE, City Sundries, 104 N. Washington. 785.546.2234. Monday-Friday 10 a.m.-7 p.m.; Saturday 10 a.m.-6 p.m.; Sunday 12-6 p.m. 1901 fountain with marble counter, back bar, and mirror; three ice cream tables.

MERRIAM, Georgetown Pharmacy Old-Fashioned Soda Fountain & Espresso Shop, 5605 Merriam Drive. 913.362.0313. Monday-Friday 9 a.m.-6 p.m.; Saturday 9 a.m.-1 p.m. Six-stool 1890 fountain with 1930 "bobtail"; syrups and carbonation added separately.

NORWICH, Redz, 246 N. Main. 620.478.2401. Monday-Wednesday 10:30 a.m.-2 p.m.; Thursday-Saturday 10:30 a.m.-7:30 p.m. Six-stool fountain with modern counter and early 1900s back bar and mirror.

OSKALOOSA, Parker's Pharmacy, 321 Jefferson. 785.863.2200. Monday-Saturday 9 a.m.-5 p.m. 1950s nine-stool fountain.

QUINTER, Ray's Pharmacy, 414 Main. 785.754.3312. Monday-Friday 9 a.m.-6 p.m.; Saturday 9 a.m.-12 p.m. 1948 13-stool fountain with brass foot rail and 1904 back bar and mirror.

SABETHA, Sabetha Healthmart Pharmacy, 934 Main. 785.284.3414. Monday-Friday 8:30 a.m.-6 p.m.; Saturday 8:30 a.m-1 p.m. Seven-stool Formica counter with back bar and mirror.

SENECA, Cornerstone Coffee Haus, 5th and Main. 785.294.0924. Memorial Day to Labor Day, Monday-Thursday 7 a.m.-5 p.m.; Friday-Saturday 7 a.m.-10 p.m.; remainder of year, Monday-Saturday 7 a.m.-5 p.m. 1950s 18-stool double-horseshoe counter.

SENECA, Rogers & Son Electric, 418 Main. 785.336.6505. Monday-Friday 8 a.m.-5 p.m.; Saturday 9 a.m.-1:30 p.m. Four-stool fountain with glass case and original 1950s Coca Cola machine.

TOPEKA, Potwin Drug Store (within Old Prairie Town at Ward-Meade Historic Site), 124 NW Fillmore. 785.368.3888. Monday-Saturday 10 a.m.-4 p.m.; Sunday 12-4 p.m.; January to March, Thursday-Saturday 10 a.m.-4 p.m.; Sunday 12-4 p.m. 1902 four-stool fountain with mirror and marble counter.

WAKEENEY, Gibson Health Mart, N. Main. 785.743.5753. Monday-Friday 9 a.m.-6 p.m.; Saturday 9 a.m.-1 p.m. 1892 nine-stool fountain with chrome spigots and modern Formica counter.

WESTMORELAND, Hoffman Pharmacy, 402 Main. 785.457.3611. Monday-Friday 8 a.m.-4:30 p.m.; Saturday 8-11:30 a.m. 1950s eight-stool fountain with Formica counter and authentic booths.

WICHITA, Jimmie's Diner, 3111 N. Rock Road. 316.636.1818. Sunday-Thursday 5:30 a.m.-10 p.m.; Friday-Saturday 5:30 a.m.-midnight. 1950s reproduction diner with fountain.

WICHITA, Old Mill Tasty Shop, 604 E. Douglas. 316.264.6500. Monday-Friday 11 a.m.-3 p.m.; Saturday 8 a.m.-3 p.m. 1920s 11-stool fountain with marble counter, back bar, and brass foot rail.

Customs

RIDING A CAROUSEL,
Abilene and Leavenworth

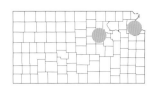

TOP 8 WONDER: *Riding a C.W. Parker Carousel is one of the 8 Wonders of Kansas Customs. Museums in Abilene and Leavenworth maintain authentic carousels and offer rides to the public.*

C.W. Parker called his carousel a Carry-Us-All as he thought that the plain term "merry-go-round" was too tame for such a flashy contrivance. It carried all ages and sizes; therefore it was a "carry-us-all."

ABILENE

Built in 1901, the carousel at the Heritage Center of Dickinson County is believed to be the oldest operating Parker carousel in existence and the third Parker carousel built. It was named a National Historic Landmark in 1987.

Totally restored, it is hand carved and features 24 horses and four chariots. A Wurlitzer 125 band organ plays while the Carry-Us-All turns. You may climb aboard this amazing invention for a ride into history.

C.W. Parker started his carousel factories in Abilene in the late 1890s. By 1905 his amusement company had four full-sized carnivals on tour. Parker died in 1932 and is buried in the family plot in Abilene.

LOCATION
412 S. Campbell,
Abilene 67401

CONTACTS
785.263.2681;
heritagecenterdk@
sbcglobal.net;
www.heritagecenterdk.com

HOURS
Labor Day to Memorial Day, Monday-Friday 9 a.m.-3 p.m.; Saturday 10 a.m.-5 p.m.; Sunday 1-5 p.m. Memorial Day to Labor Day, Monday-Friday 9 a.m.-4 p.m.; Saturday 10 a.m.-8 p.m.; Sunday 1-5 p.m. Admission charge.

explorer extras...
Also part of the Heritage Center of Dickinson County, the Museum of Independent Telephony exhibits the intriguing evolution of telephones.
ee

Customs

175

LEAVENWORTH

C.W. Parker moved his factories from Abilene to Leavenworth in 1911. The two-story factory building on 4th Street still stands. It is said that more carousels were built in Leavenworth than in any other city in the world.

The evolution of the Parker carousel is presented at Leavenworth's C.W. Parker Carousel Museum. There, young and old may ride the 1913 Carry-Us-All #118. This fully restored carousel features 24 horses, 2 rabbits, 3 ponies, a chariot, and a spinning "lovers tub." Its "stretch-style" rabbits became part of the Parker carousels after 1914.

As you ride this historic machine, original rolls of carousel music play from an Artizan band organ. Parker often used Artizan or Wurlitzer band organs to provide music for his machines. With air driven pipes, horns, drums, and cymbals, the old band organs provide a special sound reminiscent of the carousel.

LOCATION
320 S. Esplanade,
Leavenworth 66048

CONTACTS
913.682.1331;
parkermuseum@
sbcglobal.net;
www.firstcitymuseums.
org/carousel_main.html

HOURS
Thursday-Saturday
11 a.m.-5 p.m.;
Sunday 1-5 p.m.;
closed holidays
and January.
Admission charge.

explorer extras...

On average, more than 70 carved wood pieces were used to make Parker carousel figures. With a life expectancy of only five years for these fanciful animals, volunteers at the C.W. Parker Museum were masterful in restoring the 100-year-old rides. **ee**

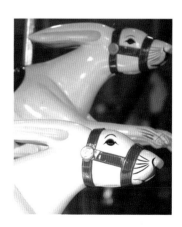

Customs

TOP 8 WONDER: *Using post rock for fencing is one of the 8 Wonders of Kansas Customs. The post-rock story is well told at the Post Rock Museum in LaCrosse.*

LOCATION
Post Rock Museum,
202 W. 1st,
LaCrosse 67548

CONTACTS
785.222.2781;
785.222.2719;
www.rushcounty.org/
postrockmuseum

HOURS
First full weekend
of May through
September,
Monday-Saturday
10 a.m.-4:30 p.m.;
Sunday 1-4 p.m.;
or by appointment.

Customs

Post rock fence posts dot the Smoky Hills region, but they are especially prominent in Lincoln, Rush, Russell, and Ellis Counties. The Post Rock Scenic Byway is a beautiful drive past many stone posts.

The limestone visible throughout the Smoky Hills is at the top of the many layers of sediment deposited by a series of interior seas that covered Kansas between 500 million and 65 million years ago.

This picturesque rock lies just below the surface of a 200-mile swath of land running southwest from a central point on the Kansas-Nebraska border to a point a few miles north of Dodge City. Post rock was very practical building and fencing material for settlers in this area during the last 25 years of the 19th century.

It is estimated that at the peak of their use, these stone post fences covered approximately 40,000 miles throughout central Kansas.

The Post Rock Museum presents the unique fence post story, including how rock is extracted from the earth using feathers and wedges. Fencing tools also are displayed.

explorer extras...

As with post rock fence posts, barbed wire played an important role in settling and fencing the plains. The Barbed Wire Museum tells this story and exhibits 3,000 different styles of barbed wire. Trade tools, including splicers, stretchers, and posthole diggers, also are displayed. Next door to the Post Rock Museum; same hours. **ee**

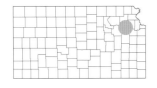

ATTENDING A COMMUNITY DINNER THEATER, Topeka

8 WONDER FINALIST: *Attending a community dinner theater is a finalist for the 8 Wonders of Kansas Customs. Audiences have been enjoying this custom at the Topeka Civic Theatre longer than anywhere else in the country.*

LOCATION
3028 SW 8th,
Topeka 66606

CONTACTS
785.357.5211;
marketing@topeka
civictheatre.com;
www.topekacivic
theatre.com

HOURS
Tours by appointment;
for show schedule
see www.topekacivic
theatre.com

Founded in 1936, Topeka Civic Theatre is the nation's oldest, continuously running community dinner theatre. It has been serving dinner and heart-warming, toe-tapping shows in the renovated 1929 Gage Elementary School since moving there in 1999. Main-stage shows range from comedies to dramas, musicals, and cutting-edge new works. In addition, children and adults provide family entertainment in Theatre for Young Audiences. Comedy "improv" is also a crowd favorite.

BUILDING WIDE MAIN STREETS, Plains

8 WONDER FINALIST: *Building wide main streets, one of the finalists for the 8 Wonders of Kansas Customs, allowed covered wagons and farm equipment to more easily navigate through a town. The widest main street in the United States is in Plains.*

LOCATION
Grand Avenue,
Plains 67869

CONTACTS
620.482.3526;
jmrroberts@hotmail.com;
www.meadecounty
ecodevo.com/widest.htm

HOURS
Always open.

Laid out in 1902, Grand Avenue is nearly a half block wide. Including the 12-foot-wide sidewalks, the street measures 155 feet, 5 inches from store front to store front. Since 1929 a raised brick sidewalk runs down the center of Grand, and cars park along either side of it as well as on both sides of the street.

CHECKING ON THE WEATHER, Harper

8 WONDER FINALIST: *Checking the weather is a finalist for the 8 Wonders of Kansas Customs. In Harper, townspeople watch the red fish weather vane at the top of the water tower for weather changes.*

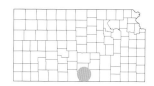

After the 125-foot stand-pipe water tower was erected in 1887, a 9 ½-foot cast iron red fish was placed at the top as a weather vane.

When a tornado hit Harper in 1892, the fish was bent double, and the pole that held it was damaged. The fish was brought down, straightened, and returned to its place.

The Biggest Fish in Kansas Flies High in Harper

The 9-foot cast-iron Fish weathervane was hoisted to the top of the 125 foot stand-pipe water tower in Sept. 1887.

An 8 Wonders of Kansas Customs Finalist

LOCATION
Main and Ash,
Harper 67058

CONTACTS
620.896.7378;
jmdollie77@yahoo.com

HOURS
Always open.

CONNECTING UNDERGROUND BUSINESSES, Ellinwood

8 WONDER FINALIST: *Connecting underground businesses is a finalist for the 8 Wonders of Kansas Customs. This practice occurred in many towns, but only in Ellinwood are the tunnels available to tour.*

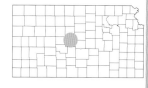

LOCATION
Tours start at Starr
Antiques, 1 N. Main,
Ellinwood 67526

CONTACTS
620.564.2400;
starrelliott@embarq
mail.com;
www.ellinwood
chamber.com

HOURS
Tours by appointment.
Admission charge.

Customs

Initially the tunnels ran through Ellinwood's entire business district and were used for coal delivery. The overlaying wooden sidewalks were lifted up; the coal was dumped in and then taken to the furnaces as needed. The advent of natural gas and an influx of population resulted in businesses building basements along the tunnels, which provided underground access. These passages also were used in imaginable ways during Prohibition. In 1982 most of the tunnels were filled with sand. Tours are conducted in those that remain.

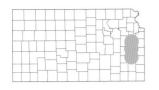

CONVERTING RAILS TO TRAILS, Ottawa to Iola

8 WONDER FINALIST: *Converting rails to trails, a popular nationwide trend, is a finalist for the 8 Wonders of Kansas Customs. The first rail-trail, Prairie Spirit Trail, opened in 1996 and now stretches 51 miles from Ottawa to Iola.*

LOCATION
Ottawa to Iola

CONTACTS
785.448.6767;
info@prairiespirittrail.org;
www.prairiespirittrail.org

HOURS
Daylight hours
outside of city limits.
Trail passes required
for persons 16 years
and older.

Built on the right-of-way of an 1860s rail line, the 8-foot-wide trail is composed of a hard-packed mixture of limestone and calcium chloride. It takes bikers or hikers through Ottawa, Princeton, Richmond, Garnett, Welda, Colony, Carlyle, and Iola, and over many bridges. Maintained by the Kansas Department of Wildlife and Parks, Prairie Spirit Trail became a state park in July 2010.

CRUISING MAIN STREET, Blue Rapids

8 WONDER FINALIST: *Cruising main street, a popular pastime, is a finalist for the 8 Wonders of Kansas Customs. It happens a little differently in Blue Rapids as kids cruise the only round town square in the state.*

LOCATION
Downtown
Blue Rapids 66411

CONTACTS
brhissoc@yahoo.com

In the early 1870s Taylor Holbrook designed the round Fountain Park as the hub of Blue Rapids. During the next 20 years, townsfolk placed a fountain in the park, planted trees around the perimeter, laid sidewalks, built a bandstand, planted hedges, and installed a soldier's memorial and flag pole. Businesses sprang up around the enclosing town square, which some cruisers have long called the "squircle."

PUTTING SHOES ON A TREE, Wetmore

8 WONDER FINALIST: *Putting shoes on a tree is a finalist for the 8 Wonders of Kansas Customs. The ritual has made a giant cottonwood near Wetmore famous as The Shoe Tree.*

In the 1970s John Kissel read about a man in another rural state who had created a shoe tree. The idea stayed with Kissel, and in the 1980s he began putting shoes on a cottonwood just north of his farm. Since boyhood, Kissel watched this tree grow to its present 23-foot diameter.

People are invited to nail shoes onto the tree or tie shoelaces together and throw a pair of shoes over a branch.

LOCATION
80th and V Road,
Wetmore 66550.
In Nemaha County, go
1 mile west of Wetmore
on K-9, 5 miles north
on W Road (blacktop),
and 1 mile west on 80th
to V Road.

HOURS
Always open.

RACING GREYHOUNDS, Abilene

8 WONDER FINALIST: *Racing greyhounds is a finalist for the 8 Wonders of Kansas Customs. The story is told at the Greyhound Hall of Fame in Abilene, the "Greyhound Capital of the World."*

LOCATION
407 S. Buckeye,
Abilene 67410

CONTACTS
800.932.7881;
info@greyhoundhallof
fame.com;
www.greyhoundhallof
fame.com

HOURS
Daily 9 a.m.-5 p.m.

Customs

Kansas was the site of the country's first official organized greyhound race. Called coursing, the first race was held near Great Bend in 1886.

Upon entering the Greyhound Hall of Fame, visitors are delighted to be greeted by a retired racing greyhound. Great dogs and leaders of the industry are honored here, and exhibits tell the colorful story of this sport.

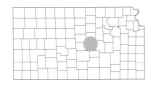

RACING MOTORCYCLES, Marquette

8 WONDER FINALIST: *Racing motorcycles is a finalist for the 8 Wonders of Kansas Customs. At the Kansas Motorcycle Museum in Marquette, antique motorcycles and racing memorabilia take visitors inside the racing culture.*

LOCATION
120 N. Washington, Marquette 67464

CONTACTS
785.546.2449;
www.ksmotorcycle
museum.org

HOURS
Daily 10 a.m.-5 p.m.;
Sunday 11 a.m.-5 p.m.

Kansas Motorcycle Museum is home to more than 100 vintage and rare motorcycles of all makes and models. The museum opened in 2003 as a tribute to Marquette's motorcycle racing legend and five-time national racing champion "Stan the Man" Engdahl. On display are more than 600 of his trophies along with his legendary custom-built Harley-Davidson that he rode during his six-decade career.

RACING ON A DIRT TRACK, Belleville

8 WONDER FINALIST: *Racing on a dirt track is a finalist for the 8 Wonders of Kansas Customs. High Banks in Belleville is the oldest continuously used dirt track in the nation.*

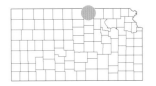

LOCATION
High Banks Hall of
Fame and Museum,
1204 H (U.S. 81
and 12th),
Belleville 66935.

CONTACTS
785.527.2526;
info@highbanks.org;
www.highbanks.org

HOURS
June through September,
Tuesday-Sunday
10 a.m.-5 p.m.;
October through May,
Wednesday-Sunday
11 a.m.-4 p.m.;
for race schedule see
www.highbanks.org

High Banks, at 1044 K, is the world's fastest half-mile dirt track. The famed track has launched many auto racing careers including those of current stars Clint Bowyer, Kasey Kahne, Jeff Gordon, and Tony Stewart.

In the 1930s the WPA built a limestone grandstand and added a banked oval to the 1910-era track.

High Banks Hall of Fame and National Midget Auto Racing Museum preserves the history of the track, the racers, and their cars.

RECITING AND CHANTING THE PSALMS, Atchison

8 WONDER FINALIST: *Reciting and chanting the Psalms is a finalist for the 8 Wonders of Kansas Customs. The Benedictine monks at St. Benedict's Abbey in Atchison perform this ritual four times a day, seven days a week.*

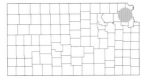

Since 1857 the monks have practiced this form of prayer, known as the Liturgy of the Hours. The liturgy combines reciting and musical chanting of the Psalms. The monks' prayer joins unaccompanied and organ-accompanied singing in unison.

The public may participate with the monks in vespers at the St. Benedict's Abbey Church at Benedictine College.

LOCATION
1020 N. 2nd,
Atchison 66002

CONTACTS
913.367.7853;
www.kansasmonks.org

HOURS
Vespers, Monday-Friday
6:45 p.m.;
Saturday 5:35 p.m.;
Sunday 5:05 p.m.

RECOGNIZING THOSE WHO CAME IN SECOND, Norton

8 WONDER FINALIST: *Recognizing those who came in second in U.S. presidential races is a finalist for the 8 Wonders of Kansas Customs and is featured at the Also Ran Gallery in Norton.*

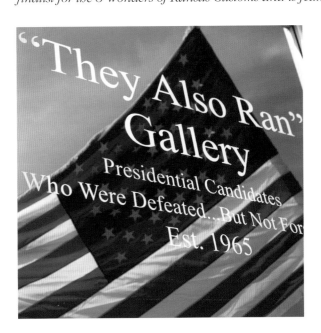

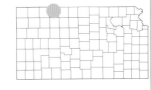

LOCATION
First State Bank,
105 W. Main,
Norton 67654

CONTACTS
785.877.3341;
theyalsoran@firststate
bank.com;
www.theyalsoran.com

HOURS
Monday-Friday
9 a.m.-3 p.m.;
or by appointment.

The gallery, inside First State Bank, exhibits portraits of unsuccessful contenders for the office of President of the United States. A short biography, a statement about the opponent, and the election year accompany each portrait.

William Walter Rouse, a former owner and president of First State Bank, started the gallery in 1965. He credits his inspiration to Irving Stone's *They Also Ran.*

Customs

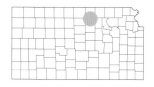

SAVING A SEAT, Concordia

8 WONDER FINALIST: *Saving a seat at the auction house is a finalist for the 8 Wonders of Kansas Customs. The seat saving has been happening in Concordia since the 1960s.*

LOCATION
220 W. 5th,
Concordia 66901

CONTACTS
785.243.3773;
785.614.2082;
kearnauction@
yahoo.com;
www.kearnauction.com

HOURS
Auctions held as
needed, usually
on a Saturday;
please call ahead.

In 1962 Clifford Sallman opened Sallman Auction House, and there folks gathered each week to chat, savor the homemade pie, and bid on treasures. In those days, each bid number was printed on a wooden paddle. Before long, paddles began showing up on chairs to save bidders' favorite seats. Since that time, the auctioneers have changed, but saving seats at the auction house (now Kearn Auction House) remains a local custom. The only difference: paddles have been replaced with pillows.

SAVING TWINE, Cawker City

8 WONDER FINALIST: *Saving twine is a finalist for the 8 Wonders of Kansas Customs and is a legendary occurrence at the world's largest (still expanding) ball of sisal twine in Cawker City.*

LOCATION
Downtown Cawker City;
south side of U.S. 24.

CONTACTS
785.781.4470;
clover@nckcn.com;
www.roadsideamerica
com/story/8543

HOURS
Always open.

Frank Stoeber started winding twine on his farm in 1953, and by 1961 his "symbol of thrift" had grown so large it was moved to Cawker City so all could see it. Visitors continue to add to the Ball of Twine, and as of January 1, 2011, it weighed 19,716 pounds and was 8,028,100 feet (or 1,520.47 miles) long!

SWIMMING IN THE SUMMER, Garden City

8 WONDER FINALIST: *Swimming in the summer is a finalist for the 8 Wonders of Kansas Customs. Garden City is home to the state's oldest continuously open and largest municipal hand-dug swimming pool.*

In 1922 Mayor H.O. Trinkle's idea for a pool became a reality through community pledges of labor, materials, and money. By today's standards, the pool is still of jaw-dropping proportions at 330 by 220 feet—larger than a football field—and it holds 2.5 million gallons of water.

A WPA bath house was built on site in the 1930s, and since that time water slides have been added. A motor boat once pulled skiers across the pool, and for a time elephants from the nearby zoo frolicked in the water after the pool closed for the season.

See an exhibit about the Big Pool at the Finney County Museum, 620.272.3664.

LOCATION
403 S. 4th,
Garden City 67846

CONTACTS
620.276.1200;
www.gcrec.com

HOURS
Summer, Monday-
Thursday 1-6 p.m.;
Friday-Sunday 1-7 p.m.
Admission charge.

WALKING TO SCHOOL, Franklin and Arma

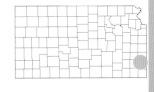

8 WONDER FINALIST: *Walking to school is a finalist for the 8 Wonders of Kansas Customs— a task made easier for students in Franklin and Arma when a sidewalk connecting the two towns was built.*

When the mining industry in southeast Kansas declined in the 1920s-1930s, businesses closed and schools downsized. Franklin schools closed forcing children to walk to and from nearby Arma. To assist the students, a three-foot-wide sidewalk was built in 1936 stretching 1.7 miles from the south edge of Arma to the south edge of Franklin. It is the world's longest sidewalk connecting two towns.

The sidewalk is listed on the National Register of Historic Places.

LOCATION
Franklin to Arma,
Crawford County.
Start at the Franklin
Community Center,
701 S. Broadway
(7th and
U.S. Business 69).

CONTACTS
franklinkansas@
yahoo.com;
www.franklinkansas.
com/sidewalkinfo.html

HOURS
Always open.

Customs

187

wonders of Kansas!
GEOGRAPHY

Geography Top 8 Wonders

Alcove Spring, near Blue Rapids

Coronado Heights, near Lindsborg

Four-State Lookout, White Cloud

Gyp Hills Scenic Drive and Gypsum Hills Scenic Byway, Barber and Comanche Counties

Konza Prairie, near Manhattan

Maxwell Wildlife Refuge, near Canton

Mushroom Rock State Park and Rock City, Ellsworth County and Minneapolis

Pillsbury Crossing, near Manhattan

Geography Finalist Wonders

Arikaree Breaks, Cheyenne County

Bartlett Arboretum, Belle Plaine

Big Basin Prairie Preserve, Clark County

Brenham Meteorites, near Haviland

Cimarron National Grassland, Morton County

Cross Timbers State Park, near Toronto

Elk River Hiking Trail, Montgomery County

Geographic Center of the United States, near Lebanon

Kaw Point Park, Kansas City

Lake Scott State Park, Scott County

Mined Land Wildlife Area, Cherokee, Crawford, and Labette Counties

Mount Sunflower, Wallace County

Native Stone Scenic Byway, Shawnee and Wabaunsee Counties

Post Rock Scenic Byway, Ellsworth, Lincoln, and Russell Counties

Schermerhorn Park, near Galena

Sternberg Museum of Natural History, Hays

Rex Buchanan, author and interim director of the Kansas Geological Survey

Take some time. Look around.

The Kansas landscape will reveal subtle but surprising variety: wooded country along the big and muddy Missouri River, the tallgrass prairie of the Flint Hills, the buffalo grass and butte-and-mesa topography of the Red Hills.

Geologists divide the state into eleven physiographic regions, places of similar terrain, from the Ozarks of southeastern Kansas and the Smoky Hills in the middle, to the High Plains out west. These places offer a range of natural experiences, accessible to just about anybody. You can watch bison and birds, admire carpets of wildflowers, or drive scenic back roads. More adventurous? Get lost in prairie grasses (both tall and short), wander through canyons, or hike rocky trails.

Kansans love of place is evident. All the 8 Wonders of Kansas Geography are remarkable. Just as amazing are the spots (such as the Cimarron National Grassland or the Arikaree Breaks) that didn't make the final eight.

Go to these places. They'll show you things you'll remember forever. They'll teach you things you'll never forget. All it takes is time.

Geography

ALCOVE SPRING,
near Blue Rapids

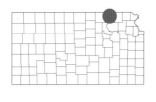

TOP 8 WONDER: *Alcove Spring is one of the 8 Wonders of Kansas Geography because of its historical significance as a stop for Indians, fur traders, and emigrants on the Oregon Trail. Wagon ruts, an intermittent waterfall, and a long-flowing spring are its main features.*

Alcove Spring was a familiar campsite near the Independence crossing of the Big Blue River. Beginning in the 1840s thousands of Oregon Trail emigrants camped near the site before fording the Big Blue and continuing west. Named in 1846 by members of the ill-fated Donner-Reed party, Alcove Spring is the final resting place for many emigrants, most notably Sarah H. Keyes, mother-in-law of James F. Reed of the Donner-Reed party. The exact location of her grave is unknown; the marker at the site, erected by the Daughters of the American Revolution in 1950, commemorates her death.

The site is well known for the waterfall near the spring. Its water is supplied by a wet weather spring, therefore the waterfall is present primarily early in the year. The many carvings on the ledge of the waterfall and rocks in the area date back to the Oregon Trail days.

Alcove Spring is on the National Register of Historic Places.

explorer extras...

To experience Marshall County's railroad history, board the custom-built passenger car on the Central Branch Railroad. The 12-mile ride takes passengers through the picturesque countryside and across a bridge trestle 85 feet above the Big Blue River. Board in Waterville or Blue Rapids. 785.363.2343; 785.799.4294; www.centralbranchrailroad.org. Reservations required. Admission charge. **ee**

LOCATION
2 miles north of
Blue Rapids on
U.S. 77, then, at the
sign for Alcove Spring,
6 miles west on
East River Road,
a gravel road.

CONTACTS
785.364.5166;
96cruisin@
embarqmail.com;
www.octa-trails.org

HOURS
Dawn to dusk.

Geography

CORONADO HEIGHTS, near Lindsborg

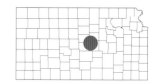

TOP 8 WONDER: *Coronado Heights is one of the 8 Wonders of Kansas Geography because it is an inspiring historic landmark and natural platform of Dakota Formation sandstone from which to observe the Smoky Valley.*

In 1541 Spanish explorer Francisco Vasquez de Coronado is thought to have explored central Kansas looking for cities of gold. Some historians believe Coronado may have used the hill known today as Coronado Heights as a lookout or encampment.

Coronado Heights is southern-most in a row of eroded sandstone hills in the area's Dakota Formation. By standing atop Coronado Heights, 300 feet above the surrounding Smoky Valley floor, visitors can see for miles—a dramatic panoramic sweep through central Kansas.

By 1920 the Lindsborg Historical Society had purchased the hill for a park, and by the following year its members had hand-dug a small road to the top. The Coronado Heights signature "castle" and picnic facilities were constructed under Roosevelt's Works Progress Administration (WPA) in 1936.

Coronado Heights is used mainly for watching wheat harvests valley-wide, witnessing first blooms of the prevalent yucca plants, cloud watching, marveling at sunset's colors, star gazing, and feeling the Kansas breeze.

explorer extras...

During the early and mid 1900s Coronado Heights was the scene of much activity, such as Bethany College dances, Fourth of July band concerts, and a number of "challenges": at least one attempt was made to roller skate down the hill, and old cars and horse-drawn wagons vied to make it to the top. **ee**

LOCATION
Coronado Heights,
3 miles north of
Lindsborg on 13th
Avenue (Coronado
Avenue), then 1 mile west
on Coronado Heights
Road. The entrance road
is just past the cemetery.

CONTACTS
888.227.2227;
785.227.8687;
info@lindsborghistory.org;
www.lindsborghistory.org

HOURS
Dawn-10 p.m.

Geography

193

FOUR-STATE LOOKOUT, White Cloud

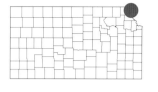

TOP 8 WONDER: *Four-State Lookout is one of the 8 Wonders of Kansas Geography because it offers a spectacular view of Kansas, Missouri, Nebraska, and Iowa from atop the rolling loess hills of the Glacial Hills region.*

LOCATION
From the main street in White Cloud, turn north across from the community park at the Four-State Lookout sign and go up the hill.

CONTACTS
Four-State Lookout, 785.595.3261; lmaysdoniphancounty@ yahoo.com; www.dpcountyks.com

HOURS
Dawn to dusk.

For decades folks have come to the hilltop to see the Missouri River below and the four states. Nebraska is three miles north of the lookout and Iowa about 60 miles north. Missouri is to the south. Sections of farmland are as much a part of the view as is the river.

In preparation for the 2004 bicentennial celebration of the Lewis and Clark Expedition, a 16-by-24-foot platform was built to elevate observers for an improved view of the valley below. Lewis and Clark signage interprets the area history.

The bluffs, composed of brown, buff, and tan loess soil, are some of the steepest in the state. The pinkish boulders often seen in the Glacial Hills fields are quartzite, an erosion-resistant rock.

explorer extras...
White Cloud was home to Wilbur Chapman, who, it is believed, was responsible for the invention of the piggy bank. The plaque at 1st and Main relates this incredible story, which begins simply with a young Wilbur (in 1913) and his pig. **ee**

Geography

GYP HILLS SCENIC DRIVE AND GYPSUM HILLS
SCENIC BYWAY, Barber and Comanche Counties

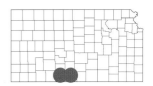

TOP 8 WONDER: *Gyp Hills Scenic Drive and Gypsum Hills Scenic Byway are one of the 8 Wonders of Kansas Geography because they vividly showcase the stunning rust-red buttes and mesas capped by layers of sparkling white gypsum.*

The Red Hills of south-central Kansas are one of the most surprising landscapes in the state. Rocks were deposited here during the Permian period, about 250 million years ago, when a large, shallow bay covered much of this area. When that bay was cut off from the ocean and the water evaporated, the remaining rocks (evaporites) included salt and gypsum. Most evaporites are easily dissolved in water, and thus erosion sculpted these hills into the shapes you see today.

Many rocks and much of the soil are stained red by iron oxide, thus giving the name Red Hills to the area. Sandstone and shale, in particular, are bright red. Gypsum, a white rock, is found in layers within those red beds. One type of gypsum, selenite, forms large diamond-shaped crystals that are common in the area and litter road cuts and ditches like broken glass.

Gyp Hills Scenic Drive

Much of this 22-mile route is through open range, meaning often there are no fences to keep cattle off the road. It is a public road with cattle guards, which are used in lieu of fences to prevent cattle from straying off property. Travelers should be sure to follow the public road and not meander off onto pasture driveways. Wildlife, native grasses, wildflowers, birds, and cattle dominate the landscape against the Red Hills.

explorer extras...

Watercolor artist Earl Kuhn's favorite subjects are the Red Hills, cowboys, and livestock. See his paintings and prints at Sagebrush Gallery, 115 E. Kansas, Medicine Lodge; 877.471.8600; www.earlkuhn.com; Monday-Friday 9 a.m.-5 p.m. Please call first. **ee**

GYP HILLS SCENIC DRIVE LOCATION
Approximately 4 miles west of Medicine Lodge on U.S. 160. At the sign reading "Gyp Hills Scenic Drive," go south on Gypsum Hill Road, then west. Watch for and follow the small green signs. Much of the route is unpaved. At about 22 miles, the route comes back north to U.S. 160 at the Lake City Road.

CONTACTS
620.886.3553; earlkuhn@sbcglobal.net

Don't be confused: the Gyp Hills Scenic Drive and the Gypsum Hills Scenic Byway are two different routes.

GYPSUM HILLS SCENIC BYWAY LOCATION
Approximately 42 miles in length, it extends from the western city limits of Medicine Lodge on U.S. 160 to U.S. 183 at Coldwater. As with the Gyp Hills Scenic Drive, you will see flat mesas, deep canyons, sharp high hills, red soils, and caprock formations. Two pull-outs along U.S. 160 provide photo opportunities.

CONTACTS
800.684.6966; 785.296.8669; travtour@ kansascommerce.com;

Geography

KONZA PRAIRIE, near Manhattan

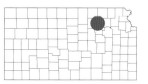

TOP 8 WONDER: *Konza Prairie is one of the 8 Wonders of Kansas Geography because it is an internationally recognized research site for tallgrass prairie ecology and because the trails offer the public a spectacular Flint Hills.*

Konza Prairie Biological Station (KPBS) is an 8,600-acre native tallgrass prairie preserve jointly owned by the Nature Conservancy and Kansas State University. The station is in the Flint Hills of northeast Kansas, a grassland region of steep slopes overlaid by shallow limestone soils unsuitable for cultivation.

KPBS, operated as a field research station by the KSU Division of Biology, is dedicated to long-term ecological research, education, and prairie conservation. It is a unique outdoor laboratory that provides opportunities for the study of tallgrass prairie ecosystems and for basic biological research.

The Flint Hills region contains the largest remaining area of unplowed tallgrass prairie in North America.

The Konza Prairie hiking trails offer visitors a selection of two-, four-, or six-mile loops. These public trails wind through lowland forest, cross Kings Creek, and climb over limestone ledges into the native tallgrass prairie.

Guided auto tours into the Konza Prairie and buffalo herd can be arranged.

explorer extras...

Find more Flint Hills adventures in Geary, Riley, and Wabaunsee Counties by taking any road off I-70 with "creek" in its name; you'll enjoy these meandering roads and the sites along the way. **ee**

LOCATION
6½ miles south on McDowell Creek Road from the K-177 intersection (just south of the Kansas River bridge on Manhattan's southeast side); or almost 5 miles north on McDowell Creek Road from I-70 exit 307.

CONTACTS
785.587.0441;
konza@ksu.edu;
http://keep.konza.ksu.edu/visit/hike.htm

HOURS
Trails open dawn to dusk.
Donations welcome.

Geography

MAXWELL WILDLIFE REFUGE, near Canton

TOP 8 WONDER: *Maxwell Wildlife Refuge is one of the 8 Wonders of Kansas Geography because its midgrass prairie provides the only place in Kansas where both buffalo and elk can be viewed in their natural habitats.*

In 1859 John Gault Maxwell drove a small buffalo herd into the present-day Canton area and set up a homestead. His dream was to preserve a piece of prairie, with a buffalo herd, for future generations. He died before he could achieve that dream, but sons John and Henry left their combined estates to make Maxwell Wildlife Refuge possible. Ten buffalo and six elk were placed at the refuge in 1951. Currently 160 buffalo and 80 elk are at home there.

The Friends of Maxwell was formed in 1993 to work with the Kansas Department of Wildlife and Parks to provide year-round tram rides to see the buffalo herd and to educate visitors about wildflowers and prairie grasses.

The only opportunity to see the elk is in the winter. From mid-September until mid-October the dominant bulls are busy gathering cows into harems. Sometimes you can hear the bugling on calm mornings or evenings.

The 4½ square miles of Maxwell Wildlife Refuge includes a public road (Pueblo Road) through the prairie that is open range. Remember, vehicles must remain on the road. Buffalo have the right-of-way.

explorer extras...

How many towns of 800 people have two water towers, much less a hot one and a cold one? This Canton oddity began as a teenage prank in the early 1960s when kids crawled to the top of one of the towers and labeled it "Hot." The city embraced the idea and painted "Cold" on the other one. **ee**

LOCATION
2577 Pueblo Road, Canton 67428. 6 miles north of Canton on K-86 (27th Avenue), then 1¼ miles west on Pueblo to Friends of Maxwell Visitor Center.

CONTACTS
620.628.4455;
maxwell@kitusa.com;
www.ck-t.com/maxwell

HOURS
Year-round tours into the buffalo herd; winter tours to view the elk. Reservations required.

Geography

201

MUSHROOM ROCK STATE PARK AND ROCK CITY,
Ellsworth County and Minneapolis

TOP 8 WONDER: *Mushroom Rock State Park and Rock City are, as a duo entry, one of the 8 Wonders of Kansas Geography because both sites showcase rare Dakota sandstone concretions deposited 100 million years ago and since exposed by the relentless forces of erosion.*

MUSHROOM ROCK STATE PARK, ELLSWORTH COUNTY

The strangely shaped rocks at Mushroom Rock State Park are made of sandstone from the Dakota Formation, deposited about 100 million years ago along the edge of a Cretaceous sea. Over time, circulating water deposited a natural cement between the sand grains, creating harder bodies of sandstone known as concretions.

Concretions are often spherical. The softer sandstone in what resembles the mushroom stem has eroded more rapidly, creating the mushroom-shaped rock.

This unique geological oddity has, over the years, drawn a variety of onlookers including Indians, mountain men, soldiers, and present-day visitors.

Until 1963 one could see these spheres only by traveling a rough trail on privately owned land. On April 25, 1965, Mushroom Rock State Park was officially dedicated as a state park.

explorer extras...
Experience the countryside near Mushroom Rock by traveling the Kanopolis Lake Legacy Trail Self-Guided Auto Tour. It showcases 27 historic sites including forts, cemeteries, and ghost towns. Brochures available at Kanopolis State Park office; 785.546.2565. **ee**

LOCATION
2 miles south and 2½ miles west of the K-140 and K-141 intersection in Ellsworth County.

CONTACTS
785.546.2565;
785.392.3068;
www.kdwp.state.ks.us

Geography

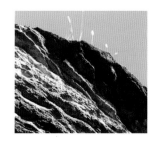

ROCK CITY, NEAR MINNEAPOLIS

Rock City, an area covered by huge sandstone spheres, is situated a few miles south of Minneapolis in Ottawa County. About 200 of these unusual rocks, ranging in diameter from 10 to 27 feet, occupy an area roughly the size of two football fields.

Known by geologists as concretions, the spheres were weathered out of Dakota Formation sandstone, which was deposited about 100 million years ago during the Cretaceous period. The spheres, formed as calcium carbonate (in the ground water), circulated through sand and cemented the sand particles around small rocks, shells, or geodes. This process caused the cemented particles to grow outward in all directions. Years of erosion have exposed some of the concretions, and probably many more remain below ground. The angled lines in the sandstone, called cross-bedding, resulted from the way the sand was originally deposited, by flowing water.

The site, owned and operated by a nonprofit corporation, has a visitor center and has been designated a National Natural Landmark.

LOCATION
1051 Ivy Road,
Minneapolis 67467.
3 miles south of
Minneapolis on K-106,
then ½ mile west on
Ivy Road.

CONTACTS
785.392.2092;
785.392.3068

HOURS
Operates as a
public park May
to September
daily 9 a.m.-5 p.m.
Admission charge.
The rocks can be
seen year round.

Geography

explorer extras...
Marking a significant event in Ottawa County history, a hilltop monument explains that Captain Zebulon Pike came through this area during his 1806 expedition. 3½ miles west of Delphos on Volunteer Road, 1½ miles south, then west on N. 52 Road. **ee**

PILLSBURY CROSSING
WILDLIFE AREA, near Manhattan

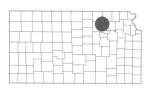

TOP 8 WONDER: *Pillsbury Crossing Wildlife Area is one of the 8 Wonders of Kansas Geography because its flat, stone creek bottom forms a natural ford that has been a landmark for generations.*

Located seven miles southeast of Manhattan, the natural flat rock crossing was named for pioneer J.H. Pillsbury, who settled in the area in 1855. The native limestone rock layer that makes up the road crossing has been used to ford Deep Creek since pre-settlement time. A 60-foot-long, five-foot-high waterfall is a few feet down river from the low-water river crossing.

During normal stream flow, you can canoe, kayak, or take a small boat a half mile upstream. Bird watching is popular and a small hiking trail is provided. Owned by the Kansas Department of Wildlife and Parks, Pillsbury Crossing is one area in the state where spotted bass occur naturally. Channel cat fish, largemouth bass, bullhead, and carp can also be found.

explorer extras...

Stories abound about people washing their Ford, Chevy, or Plymouth at Pillsbury Crossing's low-water bridge. The practice, now banned, dates to Model T days. **ee**

LOCATION
7960 State Lake Road, Manhattan 66502.
2 miles south of Manhattan on K-177 to Deep Creek Road, 3¾ miles east to where the road sharply curves south, continue east 2¼ miles on Pillsbury Crossing Road, a gravel road.

CONTACTS
785.539.9999;
www.kdwp.state.ks.us

HOURS
Daily 6 a.m.-10 p.m.

Geography

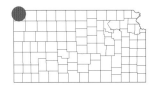

ARIKAREE BREAKS, Cheyenne County

8 WONDER FINALIST: *Arikaree Breaks is a finalist for the 8 Wonders of Kansas Geography because its deep and rugged canyons create a distinct and scenically dramatic Kansas landscape.*

LOCATION
North from the Benton and Washington intersection in St. Francis, across the Republican River bridge, and right at the first fork. A self-guided driving tour brochure is available at the Cheyenne County Museum and online at www.stfranciskansas.com, click on Area Attractions.

CONTACTS
785.332.3142;
clerk@cityofstfrancis.net

For more information, see page 44.

The Breaks were formed during the past few million years from windblown silt called loess. As water eroded loess deposits, steep-sided canyons formed.

The human environment is also present in the Arikaree Breaks. A driving tour takes visitors past the location of the Cherry Creek Encampment and other sites associated with the Sand Creek Massacre; rural schools; cemeteries; and post offices.

BARTLETT ARBORETUM, Belle Plaine

8 WONDER FINALIST: *Bartlett Arboretum is a finalist for the 8 Wonders of Kansas Geography because it is one of the oldest arboretums between the Mississippi River and the Rocky Mountains.*

LOCATION
Line and K-55,
Belle Plaine 67013

CONTACTS
620.488.3451;
info@bartlettarboretum.
com; www.bartlett
arboretum.com

HOURS
Tours by appointment;
open during events.
Donations requested.

In 1910 Dr. Walter Bartlett purchased about 20 acres to realize his passion for horticulture. Today his arboretum features hundreds of species of native and exotic trees that frame both formal and naturalistic gardens.

On the National Register of Historic Places, Bartlett Arboretum embraces 10 state champion trees, the annual Tulip Time Arts Festival, and the Tree House Concert Series. New features, botanical surprises, and ever more species of magnificent trees are continually introduced at the arboretum.

BIG BASIN PRAIRIE PRESERVE, Clark County

8 WONDER FINALIST: *Big Basin Prairie Preserve is a finalist for the 8 Wonders of Kansas Geography because it includes a mile-wide sinkhole, bison herd, and a smaller sinkhole that is home to the legendary St. Jacob's Well, a deep, funnel-shaped spring said never to have gone dry.*

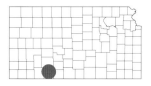

The sinkholes formed due to a process called solution-subsidence, which occurs when surface water dissolves underground deposits of salt, gypsum, or limestone.

Listed on the National Register of Natural Landmarks, St. Jacob's Well and Big Basin were once landmarks and watering sites for the Northern Cheyenne and trail drives from Texas.

LOCATION
11 miles west of Ashland on U.S. 160, then 2¾ miles north on U.S. 283; or approximately 15 miles south of Minneola on U.S. 283.

CONTACTS
620.227.8609;
www.kdwp.state.ks.us

BRENHAM METEORITES, near Haviland

8 WONDER FINALIST: *Brenham Meteorites are a finalist for the 8 Wonders of Kansas Geography because they are a rare stony-iron type, they formed the world's largest strewnfield of its kind, and they created one of only three U.S. craters authenticated by the presence of meteorites.*

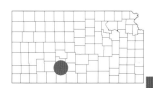

The meteorites are a single fall of a particular meteoroid an estimated 20 thousand years ago. The space rocks were named after the closest town, Brenham. The stony-iron rocks (pallasites) have an internal structure of chrome-like metal imbedded with beautiful olivine stone of yellows, oranges, reds, and greens.

LOCATION
Kansas Meteorite Museum, 21255 K, Haviland 67059. 2 miles south of U.S. 54/400 at 43rd Avenue.

CONTACTS
620.723.2318;
meteoritemuseum@gmaxx.us; www.kansasmeteorite.com

HOURS
Friday-Sunday 1-6 p.m.; or by appointment.

Geography

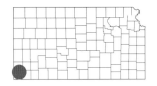

CIMARRON NATIONAL GRASSLAND, Morton County

8 WONDER FINALIST: *Cimarron National Grassland is a finalist for the 8 Wonders of Kansas Geography because of its early pioneering advancements in conservation, it contains the longest publicly owned section of the historic Santa Fe Trail, and it features three ecosystems (shortgrass prairie, sand-sage prairie, and wooded riparian).*

LOCATION
2 miles north of Elkhart on K-27.

CONTACTS
620.697.4621; sharilbutler@fs.fed.us; www.fs.usda.gov/goto/psicc/cim

For more information, see page 47.

The Soil Conservation Service developed new methods to control erosion by establishing vegetation that would provide protection. One such result was Cimarron National Grassland, which earned a national designation in 1954.

Point of Rocks, a flat-topped outcrop landmark that overlooks the Cimarron River valley, was once a lookout for Native Americans and settlers. Middle Spring was a rare reliable source of water in the area.

CROSS TIMBERS STATE PARK, near Toronto

8 WONDER FINALIST: *Cross Timbers State Park is a finalist for the 8 Wonders of Kansas Geography because it contains one of the most northern extensions of the Cross Timbers ecosystem, which includes oaks that date to 1730 and rugged sandstone-capped hills.*

This area along the Verdigris River represents a tension zone where the prairie attempts to take over the forest and vice-versa. "Ancient" Blackjack and Post oaks dominate the timber region of the 1,075-acre state park near Toronto Lake.

A mile-long trail at Cross Timbers State Park has accompanying interpretive markers.

LOCATION
144 K-105, Toronto 66777

CONTACTS
kdwp@ksoutdoors.com; www.kdwp.state.ks.us

HOURS
Always open. State park entrance charge.

ELK RIVER HIKING TRAIL, Montgomery County

8 WONDER FINALIST: *Elk River Hiking Trail is a finalist for the 8 Wonders of Kansas Geography because the 15-mile National Recreation Trail, on the edge of the Chautauqua Hills region, has been rated the best hike in the state.*

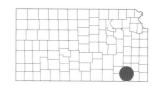

LOCATION
Elk City Lake, approximately 1 mile west of Independence, north of U.S. 160.

CONTACTS
elkcitysp
@ksoutdoors.com;
www.kansastrails
council.org

The *Hiking Guide to Kansas* by Catherine Hauber and John Young describes the trail: it "winds along a rocky ridge on the north side of the lake, travels along sheer rock walls, under rock canopies, through rock tunnels and chambers, up rock steps to bluffs overlooking the lake, and around giant boulders." Hikers will find three trailheads at Elk City Lake.

GEOGRAPHIC CENTER OF THE UNITED STATES, near Lebanon

8 WONDER FINALIST: *Geographic Center of the contiguous United States is a finalist for the 8 Wonders of Kansas Geography because this small park represents the center of the 48 contiguous states.*

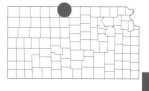

LOCATION
1 mile north of Lebanon on U.S. 281, then 1 mile west on K-191.

CONTACTS
785.389.6631

Geography

Although other locations were later named the geographic center, the site near Lebanon was unscientifically determined as such by the Coast and Geodetic Survey in 1898. A pyramidal stone monument is inscribed with the bold declaration "The Geographic Center of the United States." A local club dedicated the monument (before Alaska and Hawaii joined the Union) on June 29, 1941.

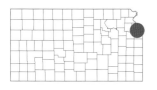

KAW POINT PARK, Kansas City

8 WONDER FINALIST: *Kaw Point Park is a finalist for the 8 Wonders of Kansas Geography because it commemorates the Lewis and Clark Expedition, which camped here in 1804, and because it provides a mesmerizing view of the confluence of the Kansas and Missouri Rivers and the Kansas City skyline.*

LOCATION
1401 Fairfax Trafficway, Kansas City. I-70 east to 3rd Street/James Street exit 423B, then 3rd to Fairfax Trafficway, and follow the Lewis and Clark signs to the Kaw Point sign.

CONTACTS
913.677.2088; mcalwell@swbell.net; www.lewisandclark wyco.org

HOURS
Always open.

The Kansas is the longest prairie-based river in the world; the Missouri, 2,533 miles in length, is the longest river in North America. On June 26, 1804, the Lewis and Clark Expedition arrived at Kaw Point, where the two rivers join, and camped for three days. Two hundred years later efforts began to preserve and interpret this portion of the historic Lewis and Clark trail.

LAKE SCOTT STATE PARK, Scott County

8 WONDER FINALIST: *Lake Scott State Park is a finalist for the 8 Wonders of Kansas Geography because of its history, its role as an oasis in an otherwise dry land, and its craggy canyons, which provide a sudden and surprising landscape on the High Plains of western Kansas.*

LOCATION
101 W. Scott Lake Drive, Scott City 67871. 10 miles north of Scott City on U.S. 83, then 3 miles northwest on K-95.

CONTACTS
620.872.2061; scottsp@ ksoutdoors.com; www.kdwp.state.ks.us

HOURS
Always open. State park entrance charge.

For more information, see page 50.

Lake Scott rests in a valley carved into the steep bluffs of the Ogallala formation. The Niobrara Chalk lies beneath the Ogallala, and water once flowed out from the contact between the two formations at the rate of 400 hundred gallons per minute.

The park offers camping, fishing, canoeing and boating, and trails for hiking and horseback riding.

MINED LAND WILDLIFE AREA,
Cherokee, Crawford, and Labette Counties

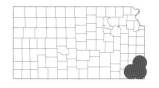

8 WONDER FINALIST: *Mined Land Wildlife Area is a finalist for the 8 Wonders of Kansas Geography because 14,500 acres of former coal mining lands have been reclaimed and now feature scenic woodlands, grasslands, and more than 1,000 strip-mine lakes.*

From the 1920s to 1974 strip-mining, the preferred method of mining coal in southeastern Kansas, cleared the ground and left deep ditches and high ridges in its wake. Before widespread land reclamation was required in 1969, much of the land once stripped of overburden, was abandoned.

Now reclaimed strip pits brimming with water and sporting a wooded environment attract birds, wildlife, birdwatchers, hunters, fishermen, and mushroom and berry pickers.

LOCATION
Example: Trout Lake, Unit 30, off U.S. 400 in Cherokee County. South on 100th NW to NW Lawton Road, then ½ mile west.

CONTACTS
620.231.3173; david.jenkins @ksoutdoors.com; www.kdwp.state.ks.us

HOURS
Always open.

MOUNT SUNFLOWER, Wallace County

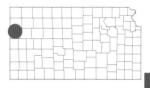

8 WONDER FINALIST: *Mount Sunflower is a finalist for the 8 Wonders of Kansas Geography because it is recognized as the highest elevation point in Kansas (4,039 feet above sea level).*

LOCATION
3 miles west of Weskan on U.S. 40, 11 miles north, 1 mile west, cross a cattle guard and continue north on a pasture driveway toward the tall dead branch.

CONTACTS
785.943.5444; www.kgs.ku.edu

HOURS
Always open.

Geography

Identified as such by the U.S. Geological Survey in 1961, this site is effectively commemorated by Ed Harold, whose family homesteaded here in 1906. The most famous attraction is the sunflower sculpture made from welded railroad spikes. The summit provides expansive vistas of the High Plains and the short-grass prairie.

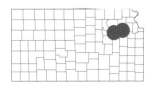

NATIVE STONE SCENIC BYWAY,
Shawnee and Wabaunsee Counties

8 WONDER FINALIST: *Native Stone Scenic Byway is a finalist for the 8 Wonders of Kansas Geography because it showcases dry-stacked stone fences and the area's native limestone out-croppings in the rolling Flint Hills.*

LOCATION
Scenic Byway, K-4 and K-99 in Shawnee and Wabaunsee Counties. Echo Cliff Park, 2 miles west and 1 mile south of Dover on K-4.

CONTACTS
800.684.6966;
785.765.4655;
www.ksbyways.org

An 1867 law abolishing the open range provided 40 cents a rod to landowners to fence their land. The native stone was so plentiful in the area that pioneers built miles of dry-stacked stone fences and many limestone buildings, all visible along this 56-mile byway. Echo Cliff Park with its large cliffs cut from native limestone is an especially scenic area.

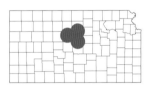

POST ROCK SCENIC BYWAY,
Ellsworth, Lincoln, and Russell Counties

8 WONDER FINALIST: *Post Rock Scenic Byway is a finalist for the 8 Wonders of Kansas Geography because it reveals dramatic limestone outcroppings, rugged Dakota sandstone bluffs at Lake Wilson, and miles of post-rock fences.*

LOCATION
North from Wilson on K-232 to K-18, then 1 mile west to Lucas.

CONTACTS
785.525.6288;
800.684.6966;
lucascoc@wtciweb.com;
www.ksbyways.org

Linking the towns of Lucas and Wilson, this 18-mile byway winds along K-232 through the Smoky Hills of north-central Kansas. The segment of the route adjacent to the Wilson Lake recreational area provides scenic turnouts that overlook the dam, lake, and valley.

SCHERMERHORN PARK, near Galena

8 WONDER FINALIST: *Schermerhorn Park is a finalist for the 8 Wonders of Kansas Geography because it represents the small part of the Ozarks that extends into Kansas and also includes the steep bluffs of Mississippian-age limestone, a 2,500-foot-long cave, and endangered species.*

In 1922 Galena resident Edgar Schermerhorn donated land on clear-running Shoal Creek for a city park. During the 1930s and 1940s the WPA built the park's well-known stone terracing walls and other structures.

Inside the park, the Southeast Kansas Nature Center provides hands-on plant and animal exhibits.

LOCATION
1½ miles south on K-26 from downtown Galena. Just before Shoal Creek Bridge, turn east into the park.

CONTACTS
620.783.5207;
lindaphipps69@ yahoo.com;
www.seksnature center.com

HOURS
Daylight hours.
Nature Center open Tuesday-Saturday 10 a.m.-4 p.m.;
Sunday 1-4 p.m.

STERNBERG MUSEUM OF NATURAL HISTORY, Hays

8 WONDER FINALIST: *Sternberg Museum of Natural History is a finalist for the 8 Wonders of Kansas Geography because its exhibits include the fossilized remains of giant fishes and marine reptiles— some of the best, most scientifically important evidence that Kansas was under water during the last half of the Cretaceous period (108 to 66 million years ago).*

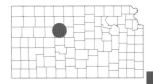

Among the Sternberg's exhibits is one of the most fascinating fossils in the world: the 14-foot "fish-within-a-fish," collected by renowned fossil hunter George F. Sternberg in 1952, just 50 miles west of Hays.

LOCATION
3000 Sternberg Drive,
Hays 67601

CONTACTS
877.332.1165;
http://sternberg. fhsu.edu

HOURS
Winter, Tuesday-Saturday 9 a.m.-6 p.m.;
Sunday 1-6 p.m.;
Memorial Day through Labor Day, Monday-Saturday 9 a.m.-6 p.m.;
Sunday 1-6 p.m.

Geography

wonders of Kansas!
HISTORY

History Top 8 Wonders

1930s Dust Bowl to Gas Exploration, Historic Adobe Museum, Ulysses

Boot Hill Museum and Historic Dodge City, Dodge City

Council Grove, a Santa Fe Trail National Landmark

Fort Scott National Historic Site, Fort Scott

Historic Fort Leavenworth, Fort Leavenworth

Historic Fort Riley, Fort Riley

Kansas Museum of History, Topeka

Kanza Tribe and Lewis & Clark's Independence Creek, Atchison

History Finalist Wonders

Black Jack Battlefield, Baldwin City

Brown v. Board of Education National Historic Site, Topeka

Cherokee Strip Land Rush, Cherokee Strip Land Rush Museum, Arkansas City

Constitution Hall State Historic Site, Lecompton

El Cuartelejo Pueblo Ruins, Scott County

Fort Hays State Historic Site, Hays

Fort Larned National Historic Site, Larned

Home on the Range Cabin, Smith County

Lead and Zinc Mining, Baxter Springs and Galena

Mahaffie Stagecoach Stop and Farm Historic Site, Olathe

Mid-America Air Museum, Liberal

National Orphan Train Complex, Concordia

Nicodemus National Historic Site, Nicodemus

Osage Catholic Mission, Osage Mission Museum, St. Paul

Pawnee Indian Museum State Historic Site, Republic County

Smoky Valley Roller Mill, Lindsborg

Leo E. Oliva, historian and writer

Kansas, located in the center of the nation, is a crossroads with a rich heritage, including Indian tribes from the East and the Great Plains, overland trails going every direction, military posts, railroads, cattle trails, cow towns, farming, ranching, mining, commerce, industry, newspapers, universities, reformers, diverse ethnic groups, and a host of others. Every one of the 105 counties offers a number of historic sites and museums to visit that help us understand what it means to be a Kansan. The historic places commemorate events that determine who we are and define the Kansas character.

The 8 Wonders of Kansas History and the 16 finalists are merely the tip of the iceberg, and the rewards of visiting the historic sites of the state are never ending. Great events happened here, many of national significance. The struggle between free-state and proslavery forces in Kansas Territory, for example, ignited the Civil War. Look around Kansas and see what gems you can find.

History

1930s DUST BOWL TO GAS EXPLORATION, Historic Adobe Museum, Ulysses

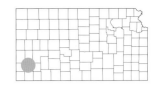

TOP 8 WONDER: *The Historic Adobe Museum's display of the 1930s, from Dust Bowl to gas exploration, is one of the 8 Wonders of Kansas History because it tells the story of human hardship to industrial boom.*

The Dust Bowl, often known as the Dirty Thirties, is said to have been the worst ecological and human disaster in modern times. The museum is in a 1938 WPA building constructed of adobe, a sign of the troubled times.

One room showcases a collection of scrap quilts, feed sack quilts, and friendship quilts to illustrate the impressive role that quilts and quilting played during the Great Depression.

A Royal Gray photo exhibit includes an image of Ulysses on Black Sunday, April 14, 1935, at 3:10 p.m., when daylight went to total darkness in one minute as the town was engulfed by dust. Gray's images, from deserted farmsteads to faces expressing every emotion, tell the story of the Dust Bowl.

Museum exhibits also tell the story of success, which started in the late 1930s when Grant County began developing its natural gas resource.

explorer extras...

At the museum, see displays about gas camps and ask for "ghost gas camp" locations around the county. **ee**

LOCATION
Historic Adobe Museum,
300 E. Oklahoma,
Ulysses 67880

CONTACTS
620.356.3009;
ulyksmus@pld.com

HOURS
Monday-Friday
9 a.m.-5 p.m.;
Saturday-Sunday
1-5 p.m.

History

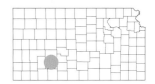

TOP 8 WONDER: *Boot Hill Museum and historic Dodge City are one of the 8 Wonders of Kansas History because the Santa Fe Trail, buffalo hunters, cattle drives, and lawmen made the city famous— then and now.*

From 1872 to 1874 an estimated 850,000 buffalo hides were shipped from Dodge City. By 1875 the buffalo herds were gone, but Texas longhorns soon took their place. From 1875 to 1886 more than five million cattle were driven up the Western Trail from Texas to Dodge City and shipped by rail to points east. During this time Dodge City was known as the "wildest, wickedest and woolliest" of the cowtowns.

Boot Hill Museum can trace its roots to the 1920s when a local doctor created a cemetery setting on the original Boot Hill Cemetery site for a Rotary convention. The Jaycees erected the first Boot Hill Museum building in 1947, and in 1958 the first buildings to replicate Dodge City's original Front Street were constructed.

The significant artifact collection at Boot Hill Museum highlights early area Native Americans, the Santa Fe Trail, Fort Dodge, the railroad, buffalo hunters, cowboys, and guns. Also presented is an exhibit about *Gunsmoke*, the popular television series set in Dodge City.

explorer extras...

Those who influenced the area's western heritage are recognized in more than 20 bronze medallions on the Trail of Fame between Boot Hill and the Santa Fe depot. An eight-foot sculpture of Wyatt Earp and a life-sized bronze of a Texas longhorn, El Capitan, *highlight the trail. Visitor Center, 400 W. Wyatt Earp Blvd., Dodge City; 620.225.8186; www.visitdodgecity.org.* **ee**

LOCATION
Boot Hill Museum,
500 Front Street,
Dodge City 67801

CONTACTS
620.227.8188;
info@boothill.org;
www.boothill.org

HOURS
Memorial Day to Labor Day daily 8 a.m.-8 p.m.; Labor Day to Memorial Day, Monday-Saturday 9 a.m.-5 p.m.; Sunday 1-5 p.m. Admission charge.

History

COUNCIL GROVE, A SANTA FE TRAIL NATIONAL HISTORIC LANDMARK

TOP 8 WONDER: *Council Grove is one of the 8 Wonders of Kansas History because it is a Santa Fe Trail National Historic Landmark town and is the site of an 1825 treaty that led to the intersection of Kaw Native American and Euro-American cultures.*

Council Grove is one of the most historic places on America's first international highway of trade, the Santa Fe Trail, a 900-mile-long road stretching from central Missouri to Santa Fe. Here, from 1825 until 1866, freighters would rendezvous in a beautiful and extensive hardwood grove on the Neosho River, organize their wagon trains, make repairs, gather supplies, then push west across the plains.

During this time Council Grove was a cultural mosaic of Mexican and Anglo traders and the Kanza (Kaw) tribe residing nearby. Today's Main Street, then the Santa Fe Trail, was a thriving commercial center, a stage for the exchange of diverse languages, customs, goods, and ideas of mid-19th century frontier America.

This well-preserved Main Street area is listed on the National Register of Historic Places, and 11 historic points of interest have been designated by the National Park Service as Santa Fe Trail National Historic Sites.

Source: Kaw Mission State Historic Site

explorer extras...

Trail Days Cafe and Museum is in an 1861 stone home that was the last house wagons passed before continuing West on the Santa Fe Trail. Today, Native American and early-settler-style foods (made from scratch) are served in 1860s, Victorian-style surroundings. 803 W. Main, Council Grove; 620.767.7986; www.traildayscafeandmuseum.org; Tuesday-Saturday 11 a.m.-8 p.m. **ee**

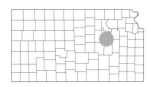

LOCATION
Self-guided tour brochures available at 207 E. Main, Council Grove 66846

CONTACTS
800.732.9211;
kawmission@kshs.org;
www.councilgrove.com

History

223

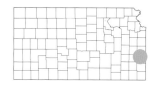

TOP 8 WONDER: *Fort Scott National Historic Site is one of the 8 Wonders of Kansas History because Fort Scott, as a U.S. Army post, had unique and important roles in the western expansion of the nation and in the Bleeding Kansas and Civil War eras.*

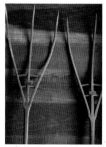

The Fort Scott military post was established in 1842. Its mission was to protect the western U.S. boundary and to police the "Permanent Indian Frontier." Troops stationed at Fort Scott also provided escort duty on the Santa Fe Trail and participated in the Mexican War.

Opening Kansas Territory to white settlement in 1854 eliminated the fort's purpose. Its buildings, auctioned to settlers in 1855, became the scene of Bleeding Kansas intrigue between proslavery and free-state factions.

When the Civil War erupted in 1861, the army returned to the town of Fort Scott, renting many buildings it previously had sold. The fort became a major Union supply and training depot, army hospital, and refugee center.

When peace returned, the army again abandoned Fort Scott. In the 1950s a group of citizens began to restore the old military post to its original appearance, and in 1978 Congress established

Fort Scott National Historic Site. The interpretation of the site includes 11 original structures and nine reconstructions.

explorer extras...

A guided trolley tour points out grave sites of Confederate soldiers, U.S. colored troops, Native American soldiers, and buffalo soldiers, as well as memorials to soldiers lost in war. Fort Scott National Cemetery, 900 E. National, Fort Scott; 620.223.2840; www.fortscott.com/trolley.php. **ee**

LOCATION
101 Old Fort Boulevard,
Fort Scott 66701

CONTACTS
620.223.0310;
FOSC_Superintendent@
nps.gov;
www.nps.gov/fosc

HOURS
April to October daily
8 a.m.-5 p.m.;
November to March
daily 9 a.m.-5 p.m.;
closed major holidays.
Admission charge.

History

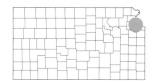

TOP 8 WONDER: *Historic Fort Leavenworth, established as Cantonment Leavenworth in 1827, is one of the 8 Wonders of Kansas History because it is the oldest continuously active U.S. Army post west of the Mississippi River, and because it is historically known as the "intellectual center of the Army."*

Colonel Henry Leavenworth founded the fort to protect the western frontier and to keep peace among Indian tribes resettled into this area. In 1829 troops began escorting traders on the Santa Fe Trail, and by the 1840s emigrant travel to Oregon and California also required military escort. Thousands of wagons passed through Fort Leavenworth as they headed west.

During the Civil War, Fort Leavenworth was an important command and control headquarters as well as a major trans-shipment point for western supplies to the East.

Fort Leavenworth is still an active military post and is home of the Command and General Staff College, considered the finest senior tactical school in the world for U.S. and international officers.

Visitors may come on post to visit historical attractions such as the Frontier Army Museum, the Buffalo Soldier Monument, and Fort Leavenworth National Cemetery. Visitors also may drive by the 1908 post headquarters, the oldest continuously occupied residence in Kansas (known as the Rookery and built in 1832), and other historic officers' quarters.

explorer extras...

Portraits and biographies of honored soldiers who trained at Fort Leavenworth are exhibited in the Fort Leavenworth Hall of Fame and in the International Hall of Fame, both inside the Lewis and Clark Center, 100 Stimson Avenue, Fort Leavenworth; 913.684.5604; leav-atzlpao@ conus.army.mil; Monday-Friday 8 a.m.-8 p.m.; Saturday-Sunday 8 a.m.-5 p.m. **ee**

LOCATION
Frontier Army Museum, 100 Reynolds, Fort Leavenworth 66027. Enter the fort at Metropolitan and 7th. All vehicles are subject to search, and photo identification is required of anyone over the age of 16.

CONTACTS
913.684.1724;
connie.cvb@visitlvks.com;
www.lvarea.com

HOURS
Outdoor self-guided tours daily 8 a.m.-5 p.m.; Frontier Army Museum, Monday-Friday 9 a.m.-4 p.m.; Saturday 10 a.m.-4 p.m.; closed national holidays.

History

227

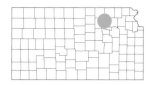

TOP 8 WONDER: *Historic Fort Riley is one of the 8 Wonders of Kansas History because the post has played a vital role in the settling and defense of our nation. Since 1917 Fort Riley has deployed troops to every war in which the United States has engaged.*

LOCATION
U.S. Cavalry Museum,
205 Custer Avenue,
Fort Riley 66442.
Enter the fort at I-70
exit 301. All vehicles
are subject to search,
and photo identification
or passport is required.

CONTACTS
785.239.2737;
william.mckale@
us.army.mil;
www.junctioncity.org

HOURS
Self-guided tours
of the post daily
8 a.m.-5 p.m.;
U.S. Cavalry Museum,
Monday-Saturday
9 a.m.-4:30 p.m.;
Sunday 12-4:30 p.m.
Tour brochures available
at the museum.

Built at the confluence of the Smoky Hill and Republican Rivers, Fort Riley was founded in 1853 to protect settlers and traders moving across Kansas to the West. The post is named for General Bennett C. Riley who, in 1829, provided the first military escort on the Santa Fe Trail.

Fort Riley played a strong peacekeeping role during the Bleeding Kansas era in the late 1850s, and after the Civil War it became a staging area for troops assigned to protect an expanding frontier.

In 1892 Fort Riley became an important fixture in the U.S. Army's educational system. Its schools served as the center for the evolution of cavalry tactics and training. Fort Riley has served as a training center during all major wars of the 20th century, and it is home to the 1st Infantry Division, the oldest division in the U.S. Army.

Fort Riley attractions include the U.S. Cavalry Museum, Custer House, 1st Infantry Division Museum, Fort Riley Cemetery, and numerous statues.

explorer extras...

A Civil War Memorial Arch, dedicated in 1898 to those who gave their lives in the war, stands in Heritage Park in downtown Junction City at 6th and Washington. The park also features a bandstand, a working fountain, and the Kansas Vietnam Memorial. **ee**

History

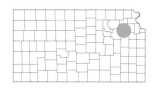

KANSAS MUSEUM OF HISTORY, Topeka

TOP 8 WONDER: *The Kansas Museum of History is one of the 8 Wonders of Kansas History because it tells the state's colorful story, including its early people, trails, settlements, Bleeding Kansas and the Civil War, trains and towns, the early 20th century, and the recent past.*

The 1880 Cyrus K. Holliday steam locomotive is the centerpiece of museum exhibits. This impressive Atchison, Topeka and Santa Fe locomotive is fully restored and is accompanied by two additional rail cars.

A full-sized Southern Cheyenne tipi and Wichita grass lodge accompany exhibits on native people who lived on the plains. The immigrant wagon and buffalo are at the center of the trails section, which features the Lewis and Clark Expedition and the Santa Fe and Oregon-California Trails. The museum's collection of Civil War flags and a howitzer are featured in the Bleeding Kansas and Civil War section.

Other museum treasures include the Queen windmill, stagecoach, log cabin, 1914 Longren biplane, and the printing press on which William Allen White printed his famous editorial, "What's the Matter with Kansas?"

The Kansas Museum of History is a division of the Kansas Historical Society, established in 1875 by the Kansas Editors' and Publishers' Association to collect and preserve present and past records.

explorer extras...

A 2½-mile nature trail on the grounds of the Kansas Historical Society provides interpretive signage about the area's cultural and natural history. Four separate trails wind visitors through woodlands, across grasslands, and along creek banks. **ee**

LOCATION
6425 SW 6th,
Topeka 66615.
Take I-70 exit 356
in west Topeka,
turn north, enter the
roundabout, and
follow the signs.

CONTACTS
785.272.8681,
ext. 401;
information@kshs.org;
www.kshs.org/
portal_museum

HOURS
Tuesday-Saturday
9 a.m.-5 p.m.;
Sunday 1-5 p.m.
Admission charge.

History

KANZA TRIBE AND LEWIS & CLARK'S INDEPENDENCE CREEK, Atchison

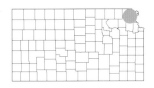

TOP 8 WONDER: *Independence Creek is one of the 8 Wonders of Kansas History because the Kanza tribe and Lewis and Clark shared this common area.*

When white explorers and traders first visited the area that would become Kansas, they encountered the Kanza tribe, who controlled much of our current state. The Kanza Independence Creek settlement was the tribe's main village as far back as 1673.

When Lewis and Clark went up the Missouri River on their historic journey through the Louisiana Purchase, they explored the Independence Creek area. Their famous landing there in 1804 occurred on July 4 — Independence Day. By coincidence, both times Lewis and Clark visited the area (July 1804 and September 1806) the Kanza were away at their buffalo hunting grounds to the west.

A re-created Kanza earth lodge at Independence Creek is on the 10-mile loop trail connecting to Atchison's Riverfront Park. An open-air pavilion at the Riverfront trailhead (Commercial and River Road) features informational panels about Lewis and Clark, the Missouri River, and the Kanza Indians.

Both the Kanza civilization and the Lewis and Clark Expedition are detailed in informational materials, artifacts, and an interactive touch screen computer at the Atchison County Historical Society Museum.

explorer extras...

Learn about Atchison's history, architecture, and commerce on the city's guided trolley tour. Board at the Visitors Center, 200 S. 10th; 800.234.1854; www.atchisonkansas.net; April through October (times vary). **ee**

LOCATION
Kanza earth lodge, 19917 314th Road, Atchison County. North on 2nd (in Atchison) past Benedictine College and Bromley Quarry, continue north on Sedgwick Road, then east on 314th Road, which winds north and east to the visitor parking lot.

CONTACTS
913.367.6238;
GoWest@
atchisonhistory.org;
www.atchisonhistory.org

HOURS
Independence Creek site open daily sunrise to sunset.

History

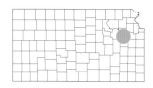

BLACK JACK BATTLEFIELD, Baldwin City

8 WONDER FINALIST: *Black Jack Battlefield is a finalist for the 8 Wonders of Kansas History because it is the site of the first regular battle between free-state and proslavery forces in Kansas, making it a significant event leading to the Civil War.*

LOCATION
163 E. 2000 Road,
Wellsville 66092.
3 miles east of Baldwin
City on U.S. 56,
and ¼ mile south
on E. 2000 Road.

CONTACTS
785.883.2106;
www.blackjack
battlefield.org

HOURS
Daylight hours;
guided tours May
through October,
Saturday-Sunday, 1 p.m.
Donation appreciated.

On June 2, 1856, a free-state militia led by abolitionist John Brown attacked a proslavery encampment near the town of Black Jack. Approximately 100 men fought an intense three-hour battle that ended with proslavery leader Henry Clay Pate surrendering to Brown.

Except for the increased number of trees, the battlefield site is still much as it was in 1856.

BROWN V. BOARD OF EDUCATION NATIONAL HISTORIC SITE, Topeka

8 WONDER FINALIST: *Brown v. Board of Education National Historic Site is a finalist for the 8 Wonders of Kansas History because it commemorates the landmark U.S. Supreme Court decision of May 17, 1954, that ended legal racial segregation in public schools.*

LOCATION
1515 SE Monroe,
Topeka 66612

CONTACTS
785.354.4273;
www.nps.gov/brvb

HOURS
Daily 9 a.m.-5 p.m.;
closed Thanksgiving,
Christmas, and
New Year's Day.

Five lawsuits from across the nation were combined as Oliver Brown et al. v. Board of Education of Topeka, Shawnee County, Kansas, et al. to challenge segregation in public education.

Designated the national historic site, Monroe School is one of four elementary schools that was set aside for black students in Topeka. Three children of Topeka plaintiffs attended Monroe, including Oliver Brown's daughter, Linda.

CHEROKEE STRIP LAND RUSH,
Cherokee Strip Land Rush Museum, Arkansas City

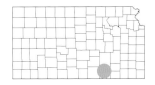

8 WONDER FINALIST: *The Cherokee Strip Land Rush, having many starting points on the southern Kansas border, is a finalist for the 8 Wonders of Kansas History because it was the largest, most spectacular, and final race for land in U.S. history.*

LOCATION
31639 U.S. 77,
Arkansas City 67005

CONTACTS
620.442.6750;
www.arkcity.org

HOURS
Tuesday-Saturday
10 a.m.-5 p.m.
Admission charge.

The opening of the Cherokee Strip to settlement brought thousands of prospective settlers to the region. By September 1893 Arkansas City's population had swelled to about 100,000, as the area teemed with land-rush hopefuls. At noon on the 16th, when the starting gun fired, the town's population dropped to 5,000, as men, women, and children raced to claim land for their own.

The story of this colorful event is told at the Cherokee Strip Land Rush Museum.

CONSTITUTION HALL STATE HISTORIC SITE, Lecompton

8 WONDER FINALIST: *Constitution Hall State Historic Site is a finalist for the 8 Wonders of Kansas History because the events that transpired inside this two-story, frame building were highly significant in igniting the Civil War.*

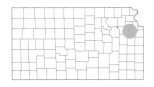

The rejected Lecompton Constitution, a proslavery document drafted in 1857, started a national firestorm. It rendered Congress and President Buchanan ineffective, fractured the National Democratic Party into antislavery northern and proslavery southern wings, and forecast huge losses for the ruling Democratic Party in the next election clearing the way for a little-known Illinois politician named Abraham Lincoln to become the first Republican president.

LOCATION
319 Elmore,
Lecompton 66050

CONTACTS
785.887.6520;
consthall@kshs.org;
www.kshs.org/portal_
constitution_hall;
www.lecompton
kansas.com

HOURS
Wednesday-Saturday
9 a.m.-5 p.m.;
Sunday 1-5 p.m.
Admission charge.

For more information, see page 47.

History

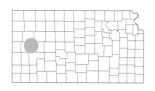

EL CUARTELEJO PUEBLO RUINS, Scott County

8 WONDER FINALIST: *El Cuartelejo Pueblo Ruins are a finalist for the 8 Wonders of Kansas History because they are archeologically significant as the northeastern-most pueblo in the United States, dating from 1650 to 1750.*

LOCATION
101 W. Scott Lake Drive, Scott City 67871.
10 miles north of Scott City on U.S. 83, then 3 miles northwest on K-95.

CONTACTS
620.872.2061; scottsp@ ksoutdoors.com; www.keystonegallery.com

HOURS
Daily 24 hours. State park entrance charge.

To escape Spanish oppression, two Pueblo bands—the Taos and the Picuris—fled in 1664 and 1696, respectively, to the plains of present Kansas. They joined their Apache allies at El Cuartelejo, a village so named by the Spanish. Plains Indians attacks in the late 1730s forced the Cuartelejo Apache south, and El Cuartelejo was abandoned.

In 1970-1971 the ruins were restored by Kansas State Historical Society archeologists. See a replicated partial pueblo at the El Quartelejo Museum, 902 W. 5th, Scott City.

FORT HAYS STATE HISTORIC SITE, Hays

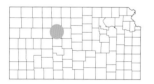

8 WONDER FINALIST: *Fort Hays State Historic Site is a finalist for the 8 Wonders of Kansas History because it was a major player in settling Kansas and the West, and its original blockhouse is one of only a few left in the nation.*

LOCATION
1472 Hwy. 183 Alt., Hays 67601

CONTACTS
785.625.6812; thefort@kshs.org; www.kshs.org/portal_ fort_hays

HOURS
Tuesday-Saturday 9 a.m.-5 p.m. Admission charge.

Founded in 1866, Fort Hays protected the railroad and white settlements in the area, and served as a major supply depot. Included in the fort's most colorful characters were Buffalo Bill Cody, Wild Bill Hickok, and George Custer. Among the well known regiments stationed here was the 10th U.S. Cavalry, whose troops became known as "buffalo soldiers."

Fort Hays became a state historic site in 1965. Four of its original buildings survive.

FORT LARNED NATIONAL HISTORIC SITE, Larned

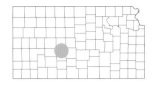

8 WONDER FINALIST: *Fort Larned National Historic Site is a finalist for the 8 Wonders of Kansas History because it is one of the best preserved authentic frontier posts in the American West.*

Established in 1859 to protect U.S. mail wagons and Santa Fe Trail traffic, Fort Larned also guarded the plains during the Civil War and Plains Indian wars.

Although founded to oppose native tribes, the post, ironically, became a site where large numbers of Indians gathered to collect annuities.

LOCATION
1767 K-156,
Larned 67550.
6 miles west of
Larned on K-156.

CONTACTS
620.285.6911;
fols_internet@nps.gov;
www.nps.gov/fols

HOURS
Daily 8:30 a.m.-5 p.m.

For more information,
see page 48.

HOME ON THE RANGE CABIN, Smith County

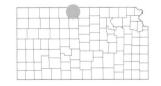

8 WONDER FINALIST: *The Home on the Range Cabin is a finalist for the 8 Wonders of Kansas History because near this site Dr. Brewster Higley wrote the words to what would become the Kansas state song.*

In 1871 Higley wrote *My Western Home*, a poem describing the beauty of his Kansas homestead. In 1873 it was printed in the *Smith County Pioneer*, and soon Dan Kelly set the poem to music; Judge John Harlan and his family first sang it publicly. The song became known as *Home on the Range* and in 1947 was named the official state song of Kansas.

The original Higley cabin still stands; Higley's poem is etched on the side of the cabin.

LOCATION
7032 90 Road,
Athol 66932.
8 miles north of Athol
on K-8, then 1 mile west
on private drive.

CONTACTS
785.695.2347;
holt@ruraltel.net

HOURS
Daylight hours.

History

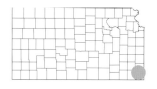

LEAD AND ZINC MINING, Baxter Springs and Galena

8 WONDER FINALIST: *Lead and Zinc Mining is a finalist for the 8 Wonders of Kansas History because from 1870 to 1945 the southeast corner of Kansas was the world's leading producer of lead and zinc concentrates.*

Lead and zinc were first discovered in southwest Missouri, and soon deposits were found in Kansas and Oklahoma. The value of this area's mineral production from 1850 to 1950 exceeded $1 billion. Eighty-one mining camps existed at one time in the tri-state area.

The southeast Kansas mining history is preserved at the museums in Baxter Springs and Galena.

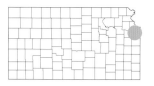

MAHAFFIE STAGECOACH STOP AND FARM HISTORIC SITE, Olathe

8 WONDER FINALIST: *Mahaffie Stagecoach Stop and Farm Historic Site is a finalist for the 8 Wonders of Kansas History because its 1865 limestone farmhouse is the only living history stagecoach stop on the Santa Fe National Historic Trail.*

In 1857 James "Beatty" Mahaffie, his wife, Lucinda, and their children arrived from Indiana in the promising new settlement of Olathe. Mahaffie's new farm was just one mile from Olathe on the Santa Fe Trail. From 1863 to 1869 the Mahaffies operated their home as a stagecoach stop on the Barlow and Sanderson Stage Line by providing meals and livery services to travelers.

Today the Mahaffie historic site offers stagecoach rides and living history programming to re-create life at a 19th-century Kansas farm and stagecoach stop.

MID-AMERICA AIR MUSEUM, Liberal

8 WONDER FINALIST: *The Mid-America Air Museum is a finalist for the 8 Wonders of Kansas History because it preserves the state's aviation history and is one of the country's largest general aviation museums.*

LOCATION
2000 W. 2nd,
Liberal 67901

CONTACTS
620.624.5263;
tourism@cityofliberal.org;
www.cityofliberal.org

HOURS
Monday-Friday
8 a.m.-5 p.m.;
Saturday 10 a.m.-5 p.m.;
Sunday 1-5 p.m.;
closed major holidays.
Admission charge.

The museum shares the stories of early flight, Kansas aviation pioneers, Wichita aircraft companies, and the planes and pilots produced in our state during World War II. A featured exhibit is of Liberal's B-24 Liberator training base, where one-third of all command pilots trained during the war. Among the museum's more than 100 vintage aircraft is a plane flown by Dwight Eisenhower, the first president who was a licensed pilot.

NATIONAL ORPHAN TRAIN COMPLEX, Concordia

8 WONDER FINALIST: *The National Orphan Train Complex is a finalist for the 8 Wonders of Kansas History because it is the nation's only museum that focuses entirely on the Orphan Train movement.*

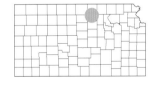

In 1850 roughly 15,000 children were homeless in New York City. They lived in alleys and under bridges where they were left to fend for themselves, join gangs for protection, and grow up in an environment of filth and violence.

In an effort to end this tragedy, the Orphan Train Program, from 1854 to 1929, placed more than 200,000 children in homes nationwide. Trains from New York carried children to all 48 continental states and into Canada. About 7,000 were placed in Kansas.

LOCATION
300 Washington,
Concordia 66901

CONTACTS
785.243.4471;
orphantraindepot@
gmail.com;
www.orphantrain
depot.com

HOURS
Tuesday-Friday
9:30 a.m.-12 p.m.
and 1-4:30 p.m.;
Saturday 10 a.m.-4 p.m.
Admission charge.

History

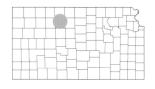

NICODEMUS NATIONAL HISTORIC SITE, Nicodemus

8 WONDER FINALIST: *Nicodemus is a finalist for the 8 Wonders of Kansas History because it is the oldest and only remaining all-black town west of the Mississippi that was established at the end of Reconstruction.*

LOCATION
304 Washington,
Nicodemus 67625

CONTACTS
785.839.4321;
www.nps.gov/nico

HOURS
Daily 9 a.m.-4:30 p.m.;
closed major holidays.

In 1877, 350 African American settlers established Nicodemus in northeast Graham County. Here they experienced real freedom and seized opportunities for self-government. Nicodemus grew from dugouts into a bustling town of limestone businesses and homes. Its heyday came in the mid-1880s when, with its hope of a coming railroad, the town grew to a population of nearly 700 and supported two newspapers, a post office, hotels, bank, livery stables, school, and churches.

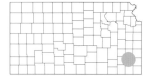

OSAGE CATHOLIC MISSION, Osage Mission Museum, St. Paul

8 WONDER FINALIST: *Osage Catholic Mission is a finalist for the 8 Wonders of Kansas History because it was one of the most important and influential early settlements in southeast Kansas.*

LOCATION
Osage Mission Museum,
203 Washington,
St. Paul 66771

CONTACTS
620.449.2320; museum@
osagemission.org;
www.osagemission.org

HOURS
Tuesday-Saturday
9 a.m.-2 p.m.

To advance Indian assimilation, religious denominations established more than 100 missions in Kansas, Missouri, Oklahoma, and Wyoming. Osage Mission, in present Neosho County, was founded in 1847 when Jesuit Fathers John Schoenmakers and John Bax, joined by the Sisters of Loretto, organized schools to educate the Osage boys and girls. When the Osage left Kansas in 1870, the schools became boarding institutions for white students from across the nation.

The mission's story is told at Osage Mission Museum.

PAWNEE INDIAN MUSEUM STATE HISTORIC SITE, Republic

8 WONDER FINALIST: *Pawnee Indian Museum State Historic Site is a finalist for the 8 Wonders of Kansas History because it is one of the only museums in the Central Plains that preserves the story and the remains of an early indigenous tribal village.*

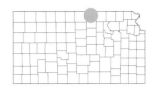

In 1901 about half of the original Pawnee site was deeded to the Kansas State Historical Society. Archeologists began excavating this 1700s village in the 1960s, and in 1967 a museum was built over the earthen floor of one of the big lodges. One of nearly 50 lodges, this round house was 50 feet in diameter and possibly housed 40 to 50 extended family members.

LOCATION
480 Pawnee Trail,
Republic 66964.
8 miles north of
U.S. 36 on K-266
in Republic County.

CONTACTS
785.361.2255;
piv@kshs.org;
www.kshs.org/portal_
pawnee_indian

HOURS
Wednesday-Saturday
9 a.m.-5 p.m.;
Sunday 1-5 p.m.
Admission charge.

For more information,
see page 51.

SMOKY VALLEY ROLLER MILL, Lindsborg

8 WONDER FINALIST: *The Smoky Valley Roller Mill is a finalist for the 8 Wonders of Kansas History because it is the oldest operational roller (flour) mill in the Midwest and the only one with all of its original equipment in place.*

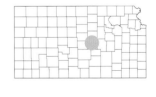

Built in 1898, the mill represents the transition to modern milling (from grinding with stones to grinding with corrugated chilled iron rolls) in Kansas in the late 19th century.

The tall brick structure not only is preserved, but is fully restored to operating condition and is able to produce flour. The mill operates (without grain) once a year during Millfest, hosted by the McPherson County Old Mill Museum the first weekend in May.

LOCATION
120 Mill,
Lindsborg 67456

CONTACTS
785.227.3595;
oldmillmuseum@
hotmail.com;
www.oldmillmuseum.org

HOURS
Monday-Saturday
9 a.m.-5 p.m.;
Sunday 1-5 p.m.;
closed major holidays.
Admission charge.

History

People Top 8 Wonders

Amelia Earhart (1897-1937), Atchison

Buffalo Soldiers, Fort Leavenworth

Carry A. Nation (1846-1911), Medicine Lodge

Emil Kapaun (1916-1951), Pilsen

George Washington Carver (1864-1943), Minneapolis and Beeler

James Naismith (1861-1939), Lawrence

Martin and Osa Johnson (1884-1937; 1894-1953), Chanute

William Allen White (1868-1944), Emporia

People Finalist Wonders

Amazon Army, Crawford County

Arthur Capper (1865-1951), Garnett and Topeka

Bernhard Warkentin (1847-1908), Newton and Halstead

Buster Keaton (1895-1966), Piqua

Clyde Cessna (1879-1954), Rago, Kingman, and Wichita

Cyrus K. Holliday (1826-1900), Topeka

Frederick Funston (1865-1917), Iola

Haskell Indian Nations University, Lawrence

Jack Kilby (1923-2005), Great Bend

John Brown (1800-1859), Osawatomie

Joseph McCoy (1837-1915), Abilene and Wichita

Mary Ann "Mother" Bickerdyke (1817-1901), Bunker Hill

Olive Ann Beech (1903-1993), Waverly and Wichita

Walter P. Chrysler (1875-1940), Ellis and Wamego

Walter "Big Train" Johnson (1887-1946), Humboldt and Coffeyville

William Inge (1913-1973), Independence

Julie Mulvihill, executive director of the Kansas Humanities Council

Historian Craig Miner once said that early in our state's history "men with beards and women in black did some serious shouting." They had something to say; a dream to pursue; a cause to further. The Kansans nominated for the 8 Wonders of Kansas People shaped our state through their voices, actions, and ideals. The list includes entrepreneurs, philanthropists, soldiers, students, adventurers, athletes, and artists. They took chances. They worked hard. Together, their stories tell us about who we are, where we've been, and what it means to be a Kansan over time and across generations. Some on the list were shouters; others dreamers. All were influential.

The stories of these Kansans teach us about our Kansas values. The list does not distinguish between those born Kansan and those who became Kansan— all come from the pages of our past. Like a favorite family heirloom passed from one generation to the next, all of us carry the responsibility of preserving these stories, sharing them with others, and adding our own to the mix. The 24 finalists form an invitation to travel the state, learn about these notable Kansans, and become inspired.

AMELIA EARHART (1897-1937), Atchison

TOP 8 WONDER: *Amelia Earhart is one of the 8 Wonders of Kansas People because she was the first aviatrix to fly solo across the Atlantic and to set many other aviation records.*

LOCATION
Amelia Earhart
Birthplace Museum,
223 N. Terrace,
Atchison 66002

CONTACTS
913.367.4217;
aemuseum@att.net;
www.ameliaearhart
museum.org

HOURS
Monday-Friday
9 a.m.-4 p.m.;
Saturday 10 a.m.-4 p.m.;
Sunday 1-4 p.m.;
December 13 to
February 13,
Tuesday-Saturday
10 a.m.-4 p.m.;
Sunday 1-4 p.m.
Admission charge.

Amelia Earhart was born in Atchison on July 24, 1897. She and her sister Muriel lived with their grandparents in Atchison until 1908 when the family moved to Des Moines, Iowa.

Amelia began flying lessons in California in early 1921. She bought her first airplane that year and broke the women's altitude record the following year.

After setting many aviation records, Amelia set out on the first around-the-world 29,000-mile flight with navigator Fred Noonan in June 1937. On July 2, after completing nearly two-thirds of the historic flight, Earhart and Noonan vanished in their attempt to land at Howland Island in the Pacific. An extensive naval, air, and land search failed to locate Earhart, Noonan, or the aircraft.

Amelia Earhart was also an author, a clothing designer, a teacher, and one of the foremost product endorsers of the time.

Today you can learn about her trend-setting life and aviation records at her grandparents' restored 1860 frame home, now the Amelia Earhart Birthplace Museum.

explorer extras...

Amelia Earhart, in the form of a life-sized bronze statue, welcomes you to the International Forest of Friendship outside of Atchison. On K-73, south of Atchison, turn right on Patriot, immediately left on Price (which becomes 278th), ¼ mile south on 278th, then ¾ mile west on 274th to Warnock Lake entrance. Both sets of Amelia's grandparents (Alfred and Amelia Otis and David and Mary Earhart) are buried at the Mount Vernon Cemetery, 2 miles south of Atchison via Price Boulevard. **ee**

People

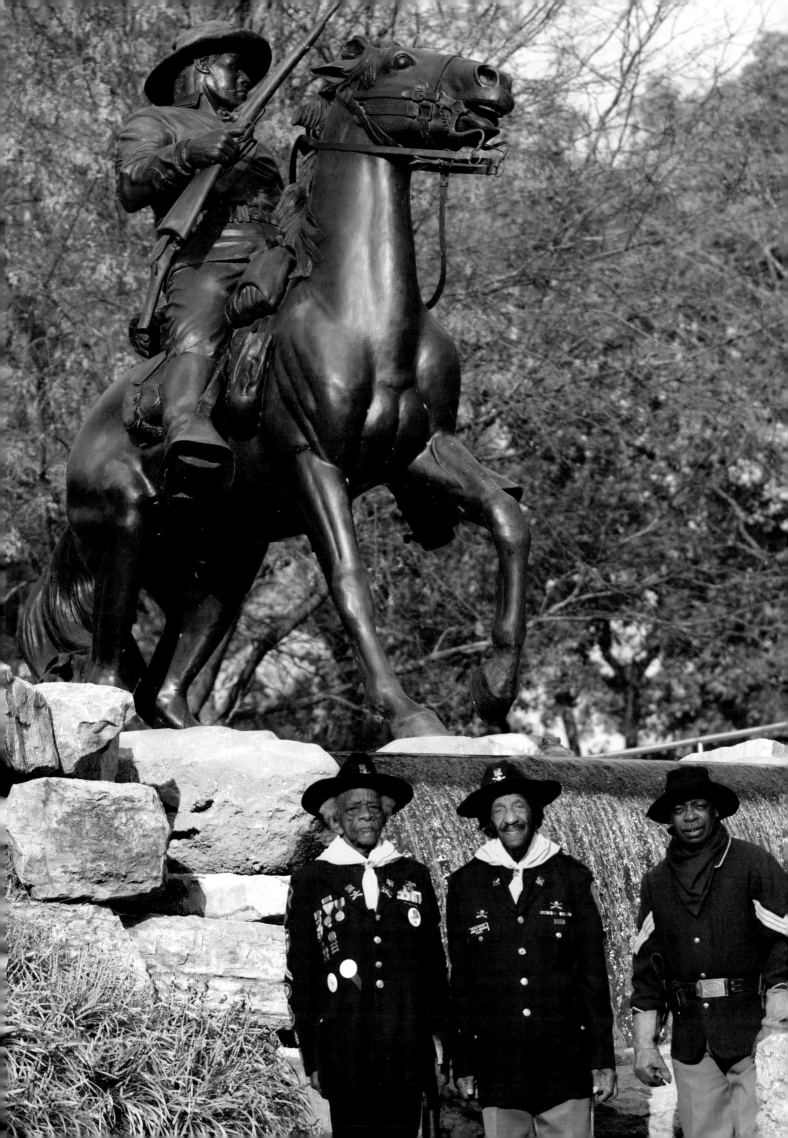

BUFFALO SOLDIERS, Fort Leavenworth

TOP 8 WONDER: *Buffalo Soldiers are one of the 8 Wonders of Kansas People because they composed one of the first all-black U.S. Army regiments, the 10th U.S. Cavalry, formed at Fort Leavenworth on September 21, 1866.*

In 1866 Congress authorized the formation of several African American regular army regiments. The first, the 9th U.S. Cavalry, was established in Louisiana, and a short time later, the 10th U.S. Cavalry was formed at Fort Leavenworth.

The 9th and 10th Cavalries and the 24th and 25th Infantries constituted the first all-black regular regiments in the U.S. Army. Although the 10th regiment was the first to be called "buffalo soldiers," the name eventually spread to signify all four African American regiments in frontier service.

The most commonly accepted theory about the name's origin is that Native Americans called the black cavalry troops "buffalo soldiers" because their dark curly hair resembled a buffalo's coat.

The Fort Leavenworth Buffalo Soldier Monument area honors these soldiers with an Eddie Dixon 13-foot bronze of a buffalo soldier astride his horse. Four busts recognize significant "firsts" in the history of African American soldiers and military units.

explorer extras...

Tours at the Richard Allen Cultural Center tell the inspiring story of General Colin Powell and Commander Carlton Philpot's efforts to create and complete the Buffalo Soldier Monument. 412 Kiowa, Leavenworth; 913.682.8772; www.richardallenculturalcenter.info/1.html; Monday-Friday 1-6 p.m.; or by appointment.
ee

LOCATION
Buffalo Soldier Monument, Grant and Stimson, Fort Leavenworth 66027. Enter the fort at Metropolitan and 7th. All vehicles are subject to search, and photo identification is required of anyone over the age of 16.

CONTACTS
913.684.1724 for a brochure about area buffalo soldier sites; connie.cvb@visitlvks.com

People

The carving of Carry A. Nation from a
cottonwood tree was loaned
by Glenn Stark, Kingman, Kansas

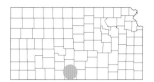

CARRY A. NATION (1846-1911), Medicine Lodge

TOP 8 WONDER: *Carry Nation is one of the 8 Wonders of Kansas People because she was a prominent crusader against alcohol and a proponent of the Woman's Christian Temperance Union during the early 1900s.*

Born in 1846 in Kentucky, sickly Carrie (later Carry) Amelia Moore grew up with her father, whom she adored, and her mother, who suffered from mental illness. By her teen years Carry had developed dominant and sometimes combative personality traits, which in part led to her obsession with moral values. In 1867 Carry married Charles Gloyd, an alcoholic, who died two years later.

In 1874 she married David Nation, a man 19 years her senior. They moved to Medicine Lodge in 1892 where David practiced law. It was there that Carry established a chapter of the Woman's Christian Temperance Union and began ardently opposing alcoholic drink.

Her adversity to alcohol was voiced initially through protest but later, and more often, through violence. Her first "raid," a passive effort, against a drinking establishment was in 1899 in Medicine Lodge. At almost six feet tall and weighing 175 pounds, Carry Nation was a formidable force as she walked into bars singing, praying with Bible in hand, and, during many protests, wielding her hatchet. She was arrested more than 30 times, and she, or her

followers, destroyed bars in some 33 Kansas towns. Her reputation was nationally known, and Carry traveled as far as England in her fight against the "demon rum."

Her husband divorced her in 1901 citing reasons of desertion. In 1903 she changed her name from her given Carrie Amelia to "Carry A. Nation," which she trademarked.

In the Carry A. Nation Home and Museum, interpretive signs provide a background of Carry's crusading life, and an imposing portrait depicts her holding a hatchet and Bible alongside her divorce decree.

explorer extras...

The famous temperance crusader is commemorated at the 1918 Carry Nation Memorial Drinking Fountain in Naftzger Park, E. Douglas and St. Francis, Wichita. And her legacy lives on at a bar counter bearing hatchet marks, supposedly a Carry Nation casualty. Idle Hour Bar, 125 E. Main, Anthony; Monday-Friday 11 a.m.-midnight; Saturday 2 p.m.-2 a.m. **ee**

LOCATION
Carry Nation Home and Museum,
211 W. Fowler
on U.S. 160,
Medicine Lodge 67104

CONTACTS
620.886.3553;
earlkuhn@sbcglobal.net;
www.kshs.org/
kansapedia

HOURS
May through November
daily 10:30 a.m.-5 p.m.;
December through April
daily 1-4 p.m.
Admission charge.

People

TOP 8 WONDER: *Emil Kapaun, a Catholic priest and military chaplain, is one of the 8 Wonders of Kansas People because of his exemplary service and dedication while held in a Korean prisoner of war camp. The Vatican currently is considering Kapaun for sainthood.*

LOCATION
St. John
Nepomucene Church,
2744 Remington Road,
Pilsen. 1 mile west of
Marion on U.S. 56,
then 8½ miles north
on Remington Road.

CONTACTS
620.924.5282;
pilsenrose@yahoo.com;
www.frkapaun.org

HOURS
Daily 9 a.m.-5 p.m.

Emil Joseph Kapaun was born on April 20, 1916, to Czech immigrants, Enos and Elizabeth Kapaun, and grew up on a farm three miles southwest of Pilsen in Marion County. In 1940 he was ordained a priest for the Diocese of Wichita at St. John's Chapel (now Newman University).

An army chaplain, he was with the United Nations forces sent to aid South Korea following the invasion by North Korea in 1950. In November of that year, Kapaun, who stayed behind with the injured from the Eighth U.S. Cavalry, was captured by North Korean and Chinese armies and sent to a prison camp.

During his incarceration, Father Kapaun displayed great courage by ministering to fellow captives regardless of the circumstances. He often disobeyed his captors' direct orders as he provided food, prayers, and other comforts to prisoners.

As he continued to aid others, his own health deteriorated, and Father Kapaun died in the POW camp on May 23, 1951. He was buried in a mass grave. Already a recipient of the Bronze Star, on

August 1951 Father Kapaun was posthumously awarded the Distinguished Service Cross.

Despite Pilsen's small population, its residents have restored St. John Nepomucene Church, where Father Kapaun held his first Mass. Near the church, an inspirational bronze statue depicts Kapaun aiding a wounded soldier during the Korean War.

explorer extras...

Next door to the St. John Nepomucene Church, the old rectory holds some Father Kapaun artifacts, and a small memorial to Kapaun stands in the cemetery behind the church. 620.924.5282; by appointment. **ee**

People

George Washington Carver:
MAN OF GOD
BY ALVIN D. SMITH

The
Peanut Man
THE STORY
OF
George Washington Carver
HARRY ALBUS

Carver Creations:
Peanuts, Sweet Potatoes and Much More

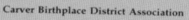

Carver Birthplace District Association

WIZARD
OF TUSKEGEE
The Life of
George Washington Carver
DAVID MANBER

GEORGE WASHINGTON
CARVER
BY RACKHAM HOLT

RACKHAM HOLT

DER
Pflanzendoktor
GEORGE WASHINGTON CARVER

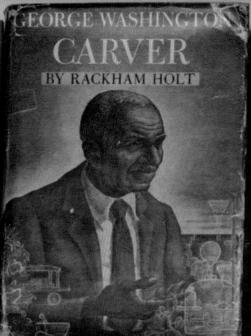

George Washington
Carver

George Washington
Carver

The REAL BOOK about
GEORGE
WASHINGTON
CARVER

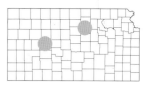

GEORGE WASHINGTON CARVER (1864-1943), Minneapolis and Beeler

TOP 8 WONDER: *George Washington Carver is one of the 8 Wonders of Kansas People because he was a highly respected agri-scientist, botanist, educator, humanitarian, and inventor, and because of his ground-breaking research in agriculture.*

Carver was born into slavery on July 12, 1864, near Diamond Grove, Missouri. Once slavery was abolished, he pursued a formal education at schools in various places, including Minneapolis, Kansas, where he attended school from 1880 to 1884 and earned his high school diploma.

Circumstances soon took Carver to Ness County, where he homesteaded near Beeler in 1886. He worked his farm for two years planting and maintaining various crops and other plants. In 1894 Carver graduated from Iowa Agricultural College, and two years later Booker T. Washington, founder of the Tuskegee Institute, convinced him to come south and serve as the school's director of agriculture.

Carver devoted his life to agricultural research. His fame primarily derives from his discovery of hundreds of new uses of crops, which he promoted to help farmers improve their quality of life. The products he derived from the peanut and the soybean revolutionized the economy of the South by liberating it from its dependence on cotton.

In Minneapolis, a sign near 2nd and Sheridan, marks the site of the school Carver attended. Additionally, the Ottawa County Museum houses a wide array of exhibits about the life of this ingenious man.

explorer extras...

In Ness County, 1 mile south of K-96 at Beeler on a gravel road, a memorial rock recognizes Carver's homestead site. Listed on the National Register of Historic Places, the memorial was erected in 1953. No buildings remain. **ee**

LOCATION
Ottawa County Museum,
110 S. Concord,
Minneapolis 67467

CONTACTS
785.392.3621;
otcomu@networks
plus.net

HOURS
Tuesday-Saturday
10 a.m.-12 p.m.
and 1-5 p.m.

People

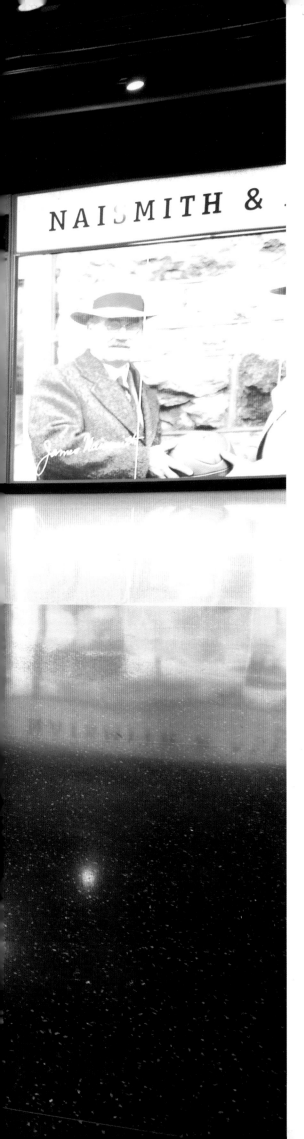

JAMES NAISMITH (1861-1939), Lawrence

TOP 8 WONDER: *James Naismith is one of the 8 Wonders of Kansas People because he is the inventor of basketball, and because in 1898 he started the University of Kansas basketball program.*

In 1891 Canadian-born James Naismith worked at the YMCA Training School in Springfield, Massachusetts. There he was challenged to create a sport that could be played indoors during the Massachusetts winters. Searching for something that required more skill than strength, and recalling the childhood game duck-on-a-rock, he invented the sport we know today as basketball.

For the first game, in 1891, Naismith used a soccer ball and two peach baskets as goals. Two years later he replaced the peach baskets with iron hoops and a hammock-style basket.

In 1898 Naismith joined the Kansas University faculty and started the school's basketball program, six years after writing the sport's first official rules. Ironically, Naismith was the only coach in the program's storied history to have a losing record (55-60).

Naismith also served as the university's athletic director, and he remained in Lawrence until his death in 1939. He is buried at Memorial Park Cemetery on East 15th in Lawrence, and a granite monument of this great man stands at his gravesite as a fitting memorial. Naismith also is honored in the Booth Family Hall of Athletics in Allen Field House.

1898: NAISMITH COMES TO KAN
nes Naismith (left, top row, far right) organize
at Kansas. The Jayhawks play their first ga
against the Kansas City YMCA team, begin
basketball. Far from the game of today, the
ow-scoring. Even so, it catches on quickly
art of KU campus life.

NAISMITH & ALLEN

THE INVENTOR
JAMES NAISMITH

LOCATION
Allen Field House,
1651 Naismith Drive,
Lawrence 66044

CONTACTS
785.864.7050;
boothhoa@ku.edu;
www.kshs.org/kansapedia

HOURS
Monday-Saturday
10 a.m.-5 p.m.
(varies on game days).

explorer extras...
Fans will recognize many names and moments in KU sports at the Booth Family Hall of Athletics in Allen Field House. Memorabilia, jerseys, trophies, and portraits of KU's best in all sports are on exhibit. 1651 Naismith Drive, Lawrence; 785.864.7050; www.kuathletics.com/facilities/ kan-booth-family-hall.html; Monday-Saturday 10 a.m.-5 p.m. **ee**

People

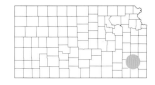

TOP 8 WONDER: *Martin and Osa Johnson are one of the 8 Wonders of Kansas People because they were pioneering wildlife filmmakers, photographers, authors, and explorers who compiled an unmatched record of exotic and distant lands.*

LOCATION
Safari Museum,
111 N. Lincoln,
Chanute 66720

CONTACTS
620.431.2730;
osajohns@yahoo.com;
www.safarimuseum.com

HOURS
Tuesday-Saturday
10 a.m.-5 p.m.
Admission charge.

Martin, raised in Lincoln and Independence, Kansas, met Osa Leighty when his traveling road show stopped in her hometown of Chanute, Kansas. The couple married in 1910, and in 1917 they made their first expedition together, traveling to the Solomon and New Hebrides Islands.

From that year until 1936 the young adventurers set up camp in some of the most remote areas of the globe and recorded life in the wildernesses of Africa, the South Seas, and Borneo. Their captivating films and photographs provided most Americans their first glimpse of these faraway places previously unknown to many. They produced 35 feature films and documentaries, some of them recording cultures and animal species that have long since disappeared.

Tragically, in January 1937 Martin died in a commercial plane crash in California. Osa, gravely injured, recovered and continued to write and publish books and films about their travels. She died in 1953.

In Chanute's Safari Museum, located in a restored 1903 Santa Fe depot, visitors can watch the Johnsons' films and view photographs and artifacts of the people and regions that Martin and Osa visited during their historic explorations.

explorer extras...
Martin and Osa Johnson are buried in Chanute's Elmwood Cemetery, between E. 10th and E. 14th and S. Malcom and S. Katy. Their graves are in section 175, block 03, lot 009. **ee**

People

257

WILLIAM ALLEN WHITE HOUSE
STATE HISTORIC SITE
KANSAS STATE HISTORICAL SOCIETY

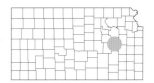

WILLIAM ALLEN WHITE (1868-1944), Emporia

TOP 8 WONDER: *William Allen White is one of the 8 Wonders of Kansas People because the Pulitzer Prize-winning "Sage of Emporia" was, as editor of the* Emporia Gazette, *a nationally known and revered voice of the American heartland for almost five decades.*

The son of a country merchant and a teacher, White was born in 1868 in Emporia. He grew up in El Dorado, where he learned the newspaper business, and he went on to work in Lawrence and at the *Kansas City Star*. In 1895 he borrowed $3,000 to purchase the *Emporia Gazette*, where he remained for the rest of his life.

In his novels, short stories, and newspaper editorials, White developed his idea of the small town as a metaphor for understanding social change and for preaching the necessity of community.

Many of his editorials became famous. The first to catapult him onto the national scene was "What's the Matter with Kansas?" Written in 1896, the piece voiced White's disgust with the Kansas political scene. In 1921, following the death of his young daughter, he poured out his grief in "Mary White," his most widely read editorial. After being arrested in a dispute over free speech he wrote "To an Anxious Friend," which won him the 1923 Pulitzer Prize.

White continued to write editorials for the *Gazette* until his death in 1944. The paper continues to be run by family.

Built in 1889, the home in which the William Allen White family lived is now a state historic site. Known as "Red Rocks" because of the red Colorado sandstone, the home is open to visitors.

explorer extras...

Many places in Emporia present a connection to William Allen White. Excerpts from his and his son's writings are found in White Memorial Park at 6th and Merchant. Peter Pan Park, at S. Rural and Kansas, was given to the city by the White family in memory of their daughter. On the southeast edge of Peter Pan Lake is a memorial featuring a bronze bust of William Allen White flanked by plaques engraved with White's moving eulogy "Mary White." William Allen White self-guided tour information is available from the Emporia Convention and Visitors Bureau, 800.279.3730. **ee**

LOCATION
William Allen White House, 927 Exchange Street, Emporia 66801

CONTACTS
620.342.2800; wawhitehouse@kshs.org; www.kshs.org/portal_william_allen_white

HOURS
Wednesday-Saturday 9:30 a.m.-5 p.m.; Sunday 1-5 p.m. Admission charge.

People

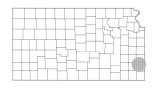

AMAZON ARMY, Crawford County

8 WONDER FINALIST: *The Amazon Army is a finalist for the 8 Wonders of Kansas People because in 1921 this group of several thousand women marched across the coalfields of southeast Kansas in courageous protest against unfair labor laws and practices.*

LOCATION
Miner's Memorial,
2nd and Walnut,
Pittsburg 66762

CONTACTS
620.231.0499;
www.amazonarmy.com

HOURS
Always open.

On December 12 at 4 a.m. between two and three thousand women—wives, sweethearts, and female relatives of striking miners—assembled at Franklin Miners Hall to begin their march to the mines. During the next three days the numbers swelled to as many as 6,000 female marchers.

This action was shocking and unheard of for women at that time and made headlines across the nation. The *New York Times* dubbed them "The Amazon Army."

Amazon Army, a mural by Wayne Wildcat, is displayed in the Pittsburg Public Library, 308 N. Walnut.

ARTHUR CAPPER (1865-1951), Garnett and Topeka

8 WONDER FINALIST: *Arthur Capper is a finalist for the 8 Wonders of Kansas People because he was the first Kansas-born governor, a 30-year U.S. senator, a newspaper and magazine publisher, and he established the Capper Fund for Children with disabilities.*

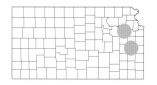

LOCATION
Easter Seals
Capper Foundation,
3500 SW 10th,
Topeka 66604

CONTACTS
785.272.4060;
www.kshs.org/
kansapedia

HOURS
Monday-Friday
8 a.m.-5 p.m.;
tours by appointment.

As a senator, Capper was instrumental in establishing legislation that created and funded 4-H. Upon his death in 1951, Capper Publishing was the largest publishing house west of the Mississippi River.

When Capper became aware of the plight of poor children with disabilities in Topeka in 1920, he immediately used his personal resources to make a difference. This beginning led to his lasting legacy, the Easter Seals Capper Foundation.

A memorial to Capper marks the site of his birth home at 5th and Cedar in Garnett.

BERNHARD WARKENTIN (1847-1908), Newton and Halstead

8 WONDER FINALIST: *Bernhard Warkentin, miller and banker, is a finalist for the 8 Wonders of Kansas People because he encouraged thousands of Mennonites from Russia to settle in south-central Kansas in the mid-1870s, and he imported and promoted Turkey red winter wheat, helping Kansas become the breadbasket of the world.*

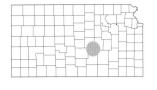

In 1885 Warkentin commissioned his nephew, Bernhard Enns, to ship several thousand bushels of Turkey red wheat seed to Newton, seed that Warkentin later distributed to local farmers at cost. With this move, Turkey red wheat immediately was available in large quantities to farmers, a significant step in the history of Kansas agriculture.

Warkentin's story is told at the Warkentin House Museum in Newton and through exhibits at the Halstead Museum, 116 E. 1st, Halstead.

LOCATION
Warkentin House,
211 E. 1st,
Newton 67117

CONTACTS
316.283.3113;
www.kshs.org/
kansapedia

HOURS
September to December and April to May, Saturday-Sunday 1-4:30 p.m.; June to August, Tuesday-Sunday 1-4:30 p.m.; closed January to March.

BUSTER KEATON (1895-1966), Piqua

8 WONDER FINALIST: *Buster Keaton is a finalist for the 8 Wonders of Kansas People because he is considered one of the greatest silent film comic actors and filmmakers.*

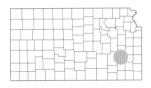

Joseph Francis "Buster" Keaton was born in Piqua in 1895 when his family was performing in the area with magician Harry Houdini.

Keaton's trademark was his deadpan expression, which earned him the nickname "The Great Stone Face." The bulk of his work occurred during the 1920s and included writing, directing, and starring in silent films. Keaton's achievements as a performer and director are widely regarded to be some of the most innovative and important in cinema history.

LOCATION
Buster Keaton Museum
(in Rural Water Office),
302 S. Hill,
Piqua 66761

CONTACTS
620.468.2385;
www.busterkeaton
museum.happywebsite.
biz/bkm-coll.htm

HOURS
Monday-Friday
9 a.m.-1 p.m.

People

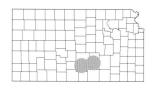

CLYDE CESSNA (1879-1954), Rago, Kingman, and Wichita

8 WONDER FINALIST: *Clyde Cessna is a finalist for the 8 Wonders of Kansas People because he was an aviation pioneer and designer and founder of Cessna Aircraft Corporation.*

LOCATION
Kingman County
Museum, 400 N. Main,
Kingman 67068

CONTACTS
620.532.3694;
620.532.5274;
www.wingsover
kansas.com

HOURS
Friday 9 a.m.-4 p.m.;
or by appointment.

Growing up in Rago, Cessna built his first airplane, the Silverwing, in 1911. During the next years he constructed monoplanes, performed exhibition flying, and started a flight school. In 1925 Cessna joined Walter Beech and Lloyd Stearman in founding Travel Air Incorporated. He left in 1927 to start Cessna Aircraft Company, and as history has shown, created a Kansas aviation legacy.

Cessna's story is preserved at the Kingman County Museum, and additionally at the Wichita-Sedgwick County Historical Museum, 204 S. Main and the Kansas Aviation Museum, 3350 S. George Washington Boulevard, Wichita.

CYRUS K. HOLLIDAY (1826-1900), TOPEKA

8 WONDER FINALIST: *Cyrus K. Holliday is a finalist for the 8 Wonders of Kansas People because he organized the Atchison, Topeka and Santa Fe Railroad and was a Topeka founder.*

LOCATION
Holliday Park and
plaque, SW 8th
and SW Western,
Topeka 66612

CONTACTS
www.kshs.org/p/
cyrus-holliday/16346

HOURS
Always open.

In 1859 Holliday secured a charter from the Kansas legislature to create a railroad, which he envisioned following the Santa Fe Trail. Federal land grants enabled construction to begin, and ground-breaking occurred in 1868. Holliday served as director of the Atchison, Topeka and Santa Fe until his death in 1900.

A Topeka founder, Holliday established the Topeka Town Association in 1854 and donated land for the state capitol grounds.

His achievements are recorded through exhibits at the Atchison County Historical Society Museum, 210 S. 10th, Atchison, and the Kansas Museum of History, 6425 SW 6th Avenue, Topeka.

FREDERICK FUNSTON (1865-1917), Iola

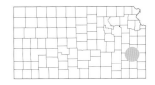

8 WONDER FINALIST: *Frederick Funston is a finalist for the 8 Wonders of Kansas People because he was the youngest brigadier general at age 35, a Medal of Honor recipient, and the "Man Who Saved San Francisco" after the earthquake and fire of 1906.*

Funston was also a botanist in Death Valley and Alaska, a soldier in Cuba, colonel of the 20th Kansas Regiment in the Philippines, and finished his career as the highest ranking officer in the U.S. Army.

A heart attack took the life of the 51-year-old general in 1917. It is believed that Funston would have been appointed the commander of the American Expeditionary Forces during World War I.

LOCATION
Allen County Museum and Boyhood Home of Frederick Funston, 20 S. Washington, Iola 66749

CONTACTS
620.365.3051;
www.allencounty
history.org

HOURS
May to October, Tuesday-Saturday 12:30-4 p.m.; November to May, Tuesday-Saturday 2-4 p.m. Admission charge.

HASKELL INDIAN NATIONS UNIVERSITY, Lawrence

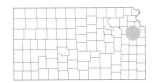

8 WONDER FINALIST: *The students of Haskell Indian Nations University are a finalist for the 8 Wonders of Kansas People because they personify how Haskell evolved from a government boarding school teaching assimilation into a university emphasizing Native American culture.*

Established in 1884, Haskell appointed its first Native American superintendent, Dr. Henry Roe Cloud, in 1933. He was a progressive educator and the first of his race to graduate from Yale University. During his time at Haskell, Dr. Roe Cloud developed the curriculum to promote and foster native culture.

LOCATION
Haskell Cultural Center and Museum, 155 Indian, Lawrence 66046

CONTACTS
785.832.6686;
www.haskell.edu

HOURS
Monday-Friday
9 a.m.-4:30 p.m.

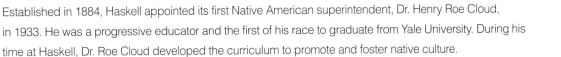

People

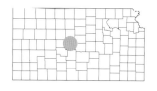

JACK KILBY (1923-2005), Great Bend

8 WONDER FINALIST: *Jack Kilby is a finalist for the 8 Wonders of Kansas People because he invented the monolithic integrated circuit, known as the microchip, which paved the way for the modern information age. He won a Nobel Prize in Physics for the invention.*

LOCATION
Barton County
Historical Museum,
85 S. 281 Highway,
Great Bend 67530

CONTACTS
620.793.5125;
www.kshs.org/
kansapedia

HOURS
Mid-April to mid-
November,
Tuesday-Friday
10 a.m.-5 p.m.;
Saturday-Sunday
1-5 p.m.
Admission charge.

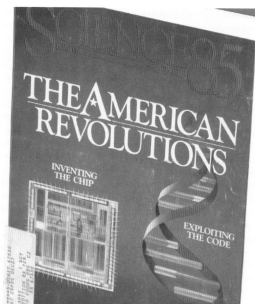

A Great Bend native, and a newly employed engineer at Texas Instruments, Kilby spent the summer of 1958 working on the circuit design problem commonly called the "tyranny of numbers." He concluded that manufacturing the circuit components en masse in a single piece of semiconductor material could provide a solution. All of our modern technology traces to Kilby's mastery of the integrated circuit.

JOHN BROWN (1800-1859), Osawatomie

8 WONDER FINALIST: *John Brown is a finalist for the 8 Wonders of Kansas People because his abolitionist crusade in Kansas had a dramatic impact on both state and national history and kept slavery in the forefront of political discussion that sparked the Civil War.*

LOCATION
John Brown Museum
State Historic Site,
1000 Main,
Osawatomie 66064

CONTACTS
913.755.4384;
www.kshs.org/portal
_john_brown

HOURS
Tuesday-Saturday
10 a.m.-5 p.m.,
Sunday 1-5 p.m.
Admission charge.

Brown came to Kansas Territory in 1855, and his actions opposing slavery included the 1856 Battle of Osawatomie. The battle occurred on the present site of the John Brown Museum.

Brown left Kansas (for the second time) in early 1859 and raided a federal arsenal at Harpers Ferry, Virginia. He was captured, tried for treason, and executed. Brown's eloquent speeches at his trial made him a martyr for the cause to end slavery.

JOSEPH MCCOY (1837-1915), Abilene and Wichita

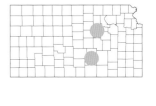

8 WONDER FINALIST: *Joseph McCoy is a finalist for the 8 Wonders of Kansas People because his innovative approach to marketing cattle on the Kansas plains in Abilene transformed a fragmented cattle business into the national industry that it is today.*

After sidetracks and stockyards were completed at Abilene in 1867, the Texas cattle route, known as the Chisholm Trail, was established. For the next four years 1.3 million cattle were driven up the trail fostering a series of Kansas cattle towns including Ellsworth, Newton, Wichita, Caldwell, and Dodge City.

McCoy is buried in Wichita's Maple Grove Cemetery, 1000 N. Hillside.

LOCATION
Heritage Center of
Dickinson County,
412 S. Campbell,
Abilene 67410

CONTACTS
785.263.2681;
www.heritage
centerdk.com

HOURS
Monday-Saturday
9 a.m.-3 p.m.;
Sunday 1-5 p.m.
Admission charge.

MARY ANN "MOTHER" BICKERDYKE (1817-1901), Bunker Hill

8 WONDER FINALIST: *Mary Ann "Mother" Bickerdyke is a finalist for the 8 Wonders of Kansas People because her heroic efforts as a Civil War nurse earned her the soldiers' great affection, and she became an avid advocate for veterans.*

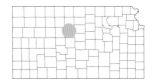

During the war, Bickerdyke gave numerous speeches across the North to solicit contributions to improve soldiers' conditions. Her "boys" named her "Mother Bickerdyke" because of her concern for them. In battle, she commonly risked her own life by searching for wounded soldiers. Following the war, her care for veterans continued, and she helped many find homes in central Kansas.

Later in life, Bickerdyke lived for several years in Bunker Hill with her son James.

LOCATION
Bunker Hill Museum,
1 block east of cafe
in a limestone church,
Bunker Hill 67626

CONTACTS
785.472.3856;
www.kshs.org/
kansapedia

HOURS
January to mid-October,
Sunday 1:30-5 p.m.;
or by appointment.

People

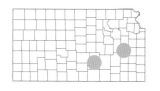

OLIVE ANN BEECH (1903-1993), Waverly and Wichita

8 WONDER FINALIST: *Olive Ann Beech is a finalist for the 8 Wonders of Kansas People because she was the first woman to head a major aircraft company and was the most successful female executive in aviation history.*

LOCATION
Wichita-Sedgwick
County Historical
Museum, 204 S. Main,
Wichita 67202

CONTACTS
316.265.9314;
www.wichitahistory.org

HOURS
Tuesday-Friday
11 a.m.-4 p.m.;
Saturday-Sunday
1-5 p.m.
Admission charge.

When Walter Beech, her husband and Beech Aircraft co-founder, began having health problems in 1940, Olive Ann Beech guided the company through the wartime production expansion. When he died in 1950, she became president of Beech Aircraft and was responsible for its diversification and joining with other companies to produce jet fighters, transports, and helicopters. Her efforts led Beech to become a powerhouse aviation company.

A historical marker honoring Olive Ann Beech is in her hometown of Waverly at 1st and Pearson.

WALTER P. CHRYSLER (1875-1940), Ellis and Wamego

8 WONDER FINALIST: *Walter P. Chrysler is a finalist for the 8 Wonders of Kansas People because he pioneered many auto industry improvements and in 1925 founded Chrysler Corporation, which became the second largest automotive company in the world.*

LOCATION
Chyrsler Boyhood
Home, 102 W. 10th,
Ellis 67637

CONTACTS
785.726.3636;
www.chryslerboyhood
home.com

HOURS
Labor Day to Memorial
Day, Tuesday-Saturday
11 a.m.-3 p.m.;
Memorial Day to Labor
Day, Tuesday-Saturday
10 a.m.-4 p.m.
Admission charge.

Hard working and always fascinated with machinery, Chrysler began his career in railroad shops. He joined the auto industry in 1910, and as a production chief for Buick, Chrysler reduced costs and modernized the company to increase output from 45 cars a day to 450.

Born in Wamego in 1875, Chrysler is featured in exhibits at the Wamego Historical Museum. When he was two years old, he moved with his family to Ellis, where his boyhood home is now a museum.

WALTER JOHNSON (1887-1946), Humboldt and Coffeyville

8 WONDER FINALIST: *Walter "Big Train" Johnson is a finalist for the 8 Wonders of Kansas People because his record-setting performances as a pitcher from 1907 to 1927 with the Washington Senators made him one of the first five players inducted into the Baseball Hall of Fame in 1936.*

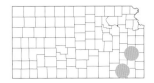

LOCATION
Dalton Defenders
Museum, 113 E. 8th,
Coffeyville 67337

CONTACTS
620.251.1194;
www.kshs.org/
kansapedia

HOURS
Daily 10 a.m.-4 p.m.
Admission charge.

Using a sweeping sidearm delivery, "Big Train" fanned 3,508 batters during a brilliant 21-year career of 417 victories with the Washington Senators. With several other unbroken records, Johnson remains the all-time career leader in shut-outs with 110.

A stone monument near Humboldt marks Johnson's birthplace. From 9th and Bridge, go two and a half miles north on the county road, then two miles west on Iowa.

Johnson maintained a part-time residence for several years in Coffeyville, where a plaque honors him at Walter Johnson Park. From U.S. 169, turn east on 8th.

WILLIAM INGE (1913-1973), Independence

8 WONDER FINALIST: *William Inge is a finalist for the 8 Wonders of Kansas People because he is a Pulitzer Prize-winning playwright who dramatized, with affection, the aspirations of ordinary people rooted in small-town life.*

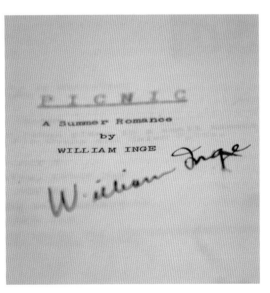

LOCATION
William Inge Collection,
Independence
Community College,
1057 W. College,
Independence 67301

CONTACTS
620.332.5492;
www.ingecenter.org/
ingecollection.htm

HOURS
During the school year,
Monday-Thursday
7:30 a.m.-9 p.m.; Friday
7:30 a.m.-4:30 p.m.;
summer, Monday-Thursday
7:30 a.m.-5 p.m.; Friday
7:30 a.m.-12:30 p.m.

Inge's *Picnic*, starring William Holden, Rosalind Russell, and Kim Novak, was filmed in several Kansas towns and won the Pulitzer Prize for Drama in 1953. Many of Inge's award-winning plays were also produced as films; among his noted works are *Bus Stop* (1955) and the film *Splendor in the Grass* (1960). The Inge Collection includes 400 of his original manuscripts.

Born in Independence, Inge attended college there and in 1935 graduated from the University of Kansas.

People

Thank you, *8 Wonders of Kansas Guidebook* supporters

The monetary support from the following guidebook sponsors and from every book purchased translates into valuable dollars for Kansas Sampler Foundation projects that preserve and sustain Kansas rural culture. To learn more about these projects please go to **www.kansassampler.org.**

$5,000

Mennonite Press, Inc., Newton

$1,000

Ellen Morgan, Salina

Ellery & Eileen Robertson, Humboldt

Emporia Convention & Visitors Bureau

Finney County Convention & Tourism Bureau, Garden City

Gene & Barb Merry, Burlington

Grant County Chamber of Commerce & Tourism, Ulysses

John & Debbie Divine, Salina

Kansas Barn Alliance (from John & Sally Hatcher, Leavenworth)

Kansas Farm Bureau, Manhattan

Wamego Telephone Communications

$500

Abilene Convention & Visitors Bureau

City of Lindsborg Department of Convention & Visitors Bureau

Clark Pharmacy/Jim and Sandi Coast, Cimarron

$500 continued

Go Wichita Convention & Visitors Bureau

Grand Central Hotel, Cottonwood Falls

Hutchinson Convention & Visitors Bureau

Jerry Kissell, Wetmore

Jim & Bonnie Miller, McPherson

Kansas Cosmosphere and Space Center, Hutchinson

Kansas Underground Salt Museum, Hutchinson

Lecompton Historical Society

Manhattan Convention & Visitors Bureau

MarCon Pies, Washington

Marion County Economic Development

Moon Marble Company, Bonner Springs

Northwest Kansas Travel Council

Rainbow Communications, Hiawatha

Sherman County Convention & Visitors Bureau, Goodland

Tri-County Telephone Association, Council Grove

WaKeeney Travel & Tourism

Wetlands and Wildlife National Byway

Index

A

Abilene 35, 46, 65, 69, 137, 171, 175, 183, 265
Abilene & Smoky Valley Railroad 65
Abraham, Eric: Flying Pig Studio and Gallery 91
Adobe House 70
Agenda 171
Aggieville 153
Alcove Spring 190-191
Aldrich Apothecary 171
All Veterans Memorial Park 167
Allen, Richard: Cultural Center 247
Allen County Museum 263
Allen Field House 255
Allen's Market building 77
Also Ran Gallery 185
Altoona 157
Amazon Army 260
American Soda Fountain and Sandwich Shoppe 173
Anchor Inn 150
Anthony 103, 171
Antonino 61
Arikaree Breaks 44, 208
Arkansas City 171, 235
Arlington 151
Arma 187
Atchison 74, 104, 156, 171, 185, 233, 245
Atchison County Historical Society Museum 233, 262
Attending a community dinner theater 180
Augusta 103

B

Badlands 27
Baldwin City 234
Ball Brothers Healthmart 171
Ball of Twine 44, 186
Ballad of the Jealous Lover of Lone Green Valley, The 98
Bankes Drug 171
Barbed Wire Museum 179
Barber County 49, 197
Bartlett Arboretum 208
Barto's Idle Hour 141
Barton County 31
Barton County Historical Museum 264
Batson's Drug 172
Baxter Springs 238
Baxter Springs Heritage Center & Museum 238

Baxter's Bait and Tackle 124
Beach Museum of Art 100
Beech, Olive Ann 266
Beeler 253
Belle Plaine 208
Belleville 98, 103, 184
Beloit 171
Benedictine College 185
Benedictine monks 185
Bennington 171
Benton, Thomas Hart 98
Bergen, Richard 63
Bickerdyke, Mary Ann "Mother" 265
Big Basin Prairie Preserve 209
Big Brutus 45, 108-109
Big Brutus Visitors Center 109
Big Pool 187
Big Well 24-25
Black Jack Battlefield 234
Blue Rapids 182, 191
Blue Sky Sculpture 84-85
Bobo's Drive In 134-135
Boelling Pharmacy 172
Bonner Springs 119
Boot Hill Museum 220-221
Booth Family Hall of Athletics 255
Bosin, Blackbear 45, 83
Bowersock Mills and Power Company 124
Bowl Plaza 91
Boyer Museum of Animated Carvings 98
Brant's Meat Market 110-111
Brenham Meteorites 209
Bringing musicians together 160-161
Brookover Feed Yards 125
Brookville Hotel 46, 136-137
Brown, John 264; Museum 264
Brown Mansion 70
Brown v. Board of Education National Historic Site 234
Buchanan, Rex: Geography, introduction by 189
Buffalo Bill bronze sculpture 86-87
Buffalo Soldier monuments 227, 247
Buffalo Soldiers 236, 246-247
Building wide main streets 180
Bunker Hill 265
Bunker Hill Museum 265
Burlington 103, 131
Bush, Martin H.: Outdoor Sculpture Collection 102

C

Caldwell 103
Caney 171
Canton 171, 201
Capper, Arthur 260; Easter Seals Foundation 260
Cardinal Drug Store 171
Carlyle 182
Carolyn's Essenhaus 151
Carver, George Washington 252-253
Castle Rock 26-27
Catharine 61
Cawker City 44, 186
Central Branch Railroad 191
Cessna, Clyde 262
Chalk Pyramids. See Monument Rocks
Chanting a school fight song 162-163
Chanute 171, 257
Chapel of the Veterans 71
Chapman, Wilbur 195
Charlie's Mexican Restaurant 151
Chase County 43
Chase County Courthouse 46, 54-55
Checking on the weather 181
Cherokee County 213
Cherokee Strip Land Rush 235
Cherokee Strip Land Rush Museum 235
Chetopa 171
Cheyenne Bottoms 30-31
Cheyenne County 44, 208
Chicken Annie's of Girard 141
Chicken Annie's Original 141
Chicken Mary's 141
Chrysler, Walter 266; Boyhood Home 266
Cimarron 171
Cimarron National Grassland 47, 210
City Sundries 173
Civil War Memorial Arch 229
Claflin 128
Clark County 209
Clark Pharmacy 171
Clicking your heels three times 164-165
Cloud Ceramics 125
Cloud County Museum Annex 125
Cobalt Boats 126
Coffeyville 70, 267
Colby 57
Colony 182
Comanche County 197

Commemorating Veterans Day 166-167
Concordia 125, 186, 239
Connecting underground businesses 181
Constitution Hall State Historic Site 47, 235
Converting rails to trails 182
Cooper Barn 56-57
Corner Pharmacy 173
Cornerstone Coffee Haus 173
Coronado Heights 192-193
Coronado Museum 165
Cottonwood Falls 46, 55, 153, 161
Council Grove 103, 147, 171, 222-223
Coutts Memorial Museum of Art 81
Cozy Inn 138-139
Crawford County 141, 213, 260
Crazy R's Bar & Grill 152
Cross Timbers State Park 210
Cruising main street 182
Curry, John Steuart: state capitol murals 50, 94-95
Custer House 229

D

Dala horses 168-169
Dalton Defenders Museum 267
Damar 75
Davis Memorial 48, 99
Deeble, Florence: Rock Garden 90
Dessin Fournir 126
Dinsmoor, Samuel P. 49, 89
Displaying an ethnic craft 168-169
Dockum Drug Store building 77
Dodge City 131, 220-221
Dole, Robert J.: Institute of Politics 149
Dreamers Awake 105
Dust Bowl to Gas Exploration 219
Dyche Hall 71

E

Earhart, Amelia 244-245; Birthplace Museum 245; earthwork of 104
Earp, Wyatt: statue 221
Echo Cliff Park 214

8 Wonders of Kansas:
    Architecture finalists 52,
    70-77; Architecture top 8
    52, 54-69; Art finalists 78,
    98-105; Art top 8 78,
    80-97; Commerce finalists
    106, 124-131; Commerce
    top 8 106, 108-123;
    Cuisine finalists 132,
    150-157; Cuisine top 8
    132, 134-149; Customs
    finalists 158, 180-187;
    Customs top 8 158,
    160-179; Geography
    finalists 188, 208-215;
    Geography top 8 188,
    190-207; History finalists
    216, 234-241; History top 8
    216, 218-233; Overall
    finalists 22, 44-51; Overall
    top 8 22, 24-43; People
    finalists 242, 260-267;
    People top 8 242, 244-259
Eisenhower, Dwight D. 35;
    Presidential Library and
    Museum 34-35
El Capitan 221
El Cuartelejo Pueblo
    Museum 236
El Cuartelejo Pueblo
    Ruins 236
El Dorado 81, 127
El Dorado Oil Field 127
Elk River Hiking Trail 211
Ellinwood 181
Ellis 61, 266
Ellsworth County 203, 214
Emma Chase Cafe 161
Emporia 167, 259
Enterprise 65
Eureka 103

Farrell, Martha Slater:
    Customs, introduction by 159
Felten, Pete: stone
    sculptures 41, 102
Finney County Historical
    Museum 125, 187
1st Infantry Division
    Museum 229
First Presbyterian Church
    of Topeka 104
5.4.7 Arts Center 25
Flint Hills National Scenic
    Byway 43
Flying Pig Studio and
    Gallery 91
Fort Hays State Historic
    Site 236

Fort Larned National
    Historic Site 48, 237
Fort Leavenworth
    226-227, 247
Fort Leavenworth Hall
    of Fame 227
Fort Leavenworth International
    Hall of Fame 227
Fort Leavenworth National
    Cemetery 227
Fort Riley 228-229
Fort Riley Cemetery 229
Fort Scott 93
Fort Scott (army post)
    224-225
Fort Scott National
    Cemetery 225
Fort Scott National Historic
    Site 224-225
Fountain Park 182
Four-State Lookout 194-195
Fox Theatre 72
Fraese Drug 172
Franklin 187
Franklin County
    Courthouse 72
Frazier, Poco: Justice 103
Fredonia 103
Free State Brewing
    Company 142-143
Fritz's Union Station 152
Fromme-Birney Round
    Barn 58-59
Frontenac 113, 141
Frontenac Bakery 112-113
Frontier Army Museum 227
Funston, Frederick 263;
    Boyhood Home 263

Gabby's Flea Market 171
Gage, Robert Merrell 63
Gage Park 135
Galena 215, 238
Garden City 77, 125, 156,
    172, 187
Garden of Eden 49, 88-89
Gardner 172
Gardner Pharmacy 172
Garnett 182, 260
Gas exploration 219
Gebhardt's Chicken and
    Dinners 141
Geographic Center of the
    United States 211
Georgetown Pharmacy
    Old-Fashioned Soda
    Fountain & Espresso
    Shop 173
Gibson Health Mart 173
Glasco 172

Goodland 103, 152
Gorham 61
Gove County 27, 29
Grand Central Hotel 153
Grant County 219
Grasshopper Company,
    The 130
Grassroots Art Center 90
Grassroots Arts Mecca of
    Lucas 88, 90-91
Graves Drug 171
Great Bend 264
Great Plains Theatre 137
"Green" Visitor Center 25
Greensburg 25
Greyhound Hall of Fame 183
Griffin Architectural Office
    building 77
Guy and Mae's Tavern
    144-145
Gyp Hills Scenic Drive 49,
    196-197
Gypsum Hills Scenic
    Byway 196-197

Halstead 103, 261
Halstead Museum 261
Hamilton 172
Harper 181
Haskell Indian Nations
    University 263
Haskell Indian Nations
    University Cultural Center
    and Museum 263
Haviland 209
Hays, Seth: home 147
Hays 61, 102, 129, 172,
    215, 236
Hays House 1857 Restaurant
    and Tavern 146-147
Hemslöjd 114-115
Herd, Stan: earthwork 104
Herington 103, 172
Heritage Center of Dickinson
    County 175, 265
Heritage Park 229
Hiawatha 48, 99
Hibachi Hut 153
High Banks Hall of Fame and
    Museum 184
Higley, Brewster 237
Hillsboro 70
Historic Adobe Museum 219
Historic Fort Leavenworth
    226-227
Historic Fort Riley 228-229
Historic Fox Theatre 72
Hodge Podge 172
Hoffman Pharmacy 173

Hoisington 103
Holliday, Cyrus K. 262;
    Park 262
Holmes Sundry 172
Holton 172
Holy Cross Church 60-61
Home on the Range
    Cabin 237
Homer's Drive Inn 154
Hope Floats 171
Horton 103
Howard 172
Hudson 121
Humboldt 267
Hutchinson 37, 39, 72, 103,
    150, 172

Idle Hour Bar 249
Independence 173, 267
Independence Community
    College 267
Independence Creek 232-233
Inge, William 267;
    Collection 267
International Forest
    of Friendship 245
International Pancake Day
    Race 165
Iola 182, 263
Irwin Potter Drug 171

Jimmie's Diner 173
John Mack Bridge 73
Johnson, Martin 256-257
Johnson, Osa 256-257
Johnson, Walter 267;
    Park 267
Johnson 173
Josie's Ristorante 154
Justice 103

Kanopolis Lake Legacy
    Trail 203
Kansas Art Collection 100
Kansas Aviation Museum 77,
    130, 262
Kansas City 152, 212
Kansas Cosmosphere and
    Space Center 36-37
Kansas Historical Society 231
Kansas Judicial Center 103
Kansas Meteorite
    Museum 209
Kansas Motorcycle
    Museum 184
Kansas Museum of History
    230-231, 262

Kansas Oil Museum 127
Kansas State Capitol 50,
    62-63, 95
Kansas Underground Salt
    Museum 38-39
Kansas Vietnam
    Memorial 229
Kansas Wetlands Education
    Center 31
Kanza Indians 233;
    earth lodge 233
Kanza Tribe and Lewis &
    Clark's Independence
    Creek 232-233
Kapaun, Emil 250-251
Kaw Point Park 212
Kearn Auction House 186
Keaton, Buster 261;
    Museum 261
Keeper of the Plains 45, 82-83
Kelley, K. Vance: Architecture,
    introduction by 53
Kendall, Dave: Cuisine,
    introduction by 133
Keystone Gallery 29
Kilby, Jack 264
Kingman 103, 262
Kingman County
    Museum 262
Kiowa County Historical
    Society 59
Koerperich Bookbinders 127
Koger Variety 172
Konza Prairie 198-199
Konza Prairie Biological
    Station 199

Labette County 213
LaCrosse 179
Lake Scott State Park 50, 212
Larned 48, 237
Lawrence 98, 124, 143, 149,
    163, 255, 263
Lawrence Visitor Information
    Center 143
Layton, Elizabeth
    "Grandma" 100
Lead and Zinc Mining 238
Leavenworth 71, 154, 173,
    175, 177
Lebanon 211
Lebold Mansion 64-65
Lecompton 47, 235
Leoti 151
Lewis and Clark Center 227
Lewis and Clark
    Expedition 212, 233
Liberal 165, 239
Liebenthal 61

Liggett, M.T.: metal
    sculptures 101
Lincoln County 214
Lindsborg 81, 101, 103, 115,
    169, 193, 241
Linger Longer 171
Linn County Courthouse 55
Loewen, Peter Paul: House 70
Loretta 61
Lucas 49, 88-91, 111
Lyon County Museum 167

Mahaffie Stagecoach Stop
    and Farm Historic Site 238
Manhattan 100, 153, 199, 207
MarCon Pies 116-117
Marquette 173, 184
Marshall County 191
Mary Queen of Peace
    Catholic Church 73
Masonic Center 74
Maxwell Wildlife
    Refuge 200-201
McCoy, Joseph 265
McPherson County Old Mill
    Museum 241
Medicine Lodge 249
Memorial Campanile and
    Carillon 163
Mercy Health Center 93
Merriam 173
Mid-America Air Museum 239
Mill Creek Antiques 128
Millers of Claflin 128
Mined Land Wildlife Area 213
Miner's Memorial 260
Minisa Bridge 77
Minneapolis 203, 205, 253
Monroe School 234
Montgomery County 211
Monument Rocks 27-29
Moon Marble
    Company 118-119
Morton County 47, 210
Mound City 55
Moundridge 130
Mount Hope Cemetery 99
Mount Sunflower 213
Mr. K's Farmhouse 35
Mri-Pilar's "Garden of Isis" 90
Muchnic Home and Art
    Gallery 74
Mulberry 141
Mullinville 59, 101
Mulvihill, Julie: People,
    introduction by 242
Munjor 61
Museum of Independent
    Telephony 175
Mushroom Rock State
    Park 202-203

Naismith, James 254-255
Nation, Carry A. 248-249;
    Home and Museum 249;
    Memorial Drinking
    Fountain 249
National Agricultural Center
    and Hall of Fame 119
National Orphan Train
    Complex 239
Native Stone Scenic Byway 214
Natural History Museum 71
Nemaha County 97
Neodesha 103, 126
Nerman Museum of Art 99
Ness, Noah V.B.: statue 67
Ness City 67
Ness City Chamber of
    Commerce 67
Ness County Bank 66-67
Ness County Courthouse 67
Newton 85, 261
Nicodemus National Historic
    Site 240
North Riverside Park Comfort
    Station 77
Norton, Charlie: *Buffalo Bill*
    bronze sculpture 86-87
Norton 185
Norwich 173
NuWay Cafe 155

Oakley 87
Olathe 85, 238
Old Jefferson Town 95
Old Mill Tasty Shop 173
Old Store 173
Oliva, Leo E.: History,
    introduction by 217
Olive Tree Bistro 155
"Open Range Zoo" 89
Ordering a soda fountain
    treat 170-173
Orphan Train Complex 239
Osage Catholic Mission 240
Osage Mission Museum 240
Osawatomie 264
Osborne 75
Osborne County Courthouse 75
Oskaloosa 95, 173
Oswego 103
Ottawa 72, 182
Ottawa County 205
Ottawa County Museum 253
Otterness, Tom:
    Dreamers Awake 105
Overland Park 99
Oz Museum 165

Pallucca's Market 113
Pancake House 165
Paolucci's Restaurant 156
Parker, C. W. 175, 177;
    Carousel Museum 177
Parker's Pharmacy 173
Parks, Gordon 92-93;
    Museum/Center for
    Culture and Diversity 93
Pawnee Indian Museum State
    Historic Site 51, 241
Paxico 128
Penner, Mil: 8 Wonders,
    introduction by 23
Perfect Pair 171
Peter Pan Park 259
Pfeifer 61
Pho Hoa Vietnamese
    Restaurant 156
Pichler's Chicken Annie's 141
Pillsbury Crossing Wildlife
    Area 206-207
Pilsen 251
Piqua 261
Pittsburg 141
Pittsburg Public Library 260
Plains 180
Plainville 126
Point of Rocks 210
Pome on the Range Orchard
    and Winery 145
Porubsky, C.W.: Deli
    and Tavern 150
Post Office Section Art 103
Post Rock fence 178-179
Post Rock Museum 179
Post Rock Scenic
    Byway 179, 214
Pottawatomie County
    Courthouse 55
Potwin Drug Store 173
Prairie Mercantile 67
Prairie Museum of Art
    and History 57
Prairie Nut Hut 157
Prairie Spirit Trail 182
Princeton 182
Putting shoes on a tree 183

Quinter 173
Quivira National Wildlife
    Refuge 31-33

Racing greyhounds 183
Racing motorcycles 184
Racing on a dirt track 184
Rago 262
RANS 129
Ray's Pharmacy 173
Raymer, Lester: Red Barn
    Studio 101
Reciting and chanting
    the Psalms 185
Recognizing those who came
    in second 185
Red Barn Studio 101
Redz 173
Republic 51, 241
Richardson, Jim: Art,
    introduction by 79
Richmond 182
Riding a carousel 174-177
Riggs Drug 171
Ring of Fire 83
Ringneck Ranch 129
"Rock Chalk Jayhawk"
    chant 163
Rock City 203-205
Roe Cloud, Henry 263
Rogers & Son Electric 173
Rookery, The 227
Russell 103
Russell County 214

Sabetha 103, 173
Sabetha Healthmart
    Pharmacy 173
Safari Museum 257
Sagebrush Gallery 197
Salina 74, 139
Samson of the Cimarron 76
Sandzén, Birger 80-81;
    Memorial Gallery 81
Santa Fe Trail National
    Historic Landmark 223
Saving a seat 186
Saving twine 186
Scammon 154
Schermerhorn Park 215
Schoenchen 61
Schonhoff Dutch Mill 165
Schuster, Harland:
    essay by 17; photos by,
    throughout
Scott County 50, 212, 236
Section Art 103
Seelye Mansion 68-69
Seelye Patent Medicine
    Museum 69

Selden 127
Seneca 103, 173
Seward County 76
Shawnee County 214
Shoe Tree 183
Silo Eco-Home 25
Simpson 157
Small World Gallery 115
Smith County 237
Smoky Valley Roller Mill 241
Soda fountains 170-173
Soda n' Suds 171
Soda Shoppe 172
Some/One 99
South Fork Spillman Creek
    Bridge 123
Southeast Kansas Nature
    Center 215
Spencer Art Museum 98
Spirit of the American
    Doughboy 87
Spirit of the Prairie 57
Spring Hill Farm and Stock
    Ranch 43
St. Bede's Parish 97
St. Benedict 51, 97
St. Benedict's Abbey 185
St. Fidelis Church 40-41
St. Jacob's Well 209
St. John Nepomucene
    Church 251
St. Joseph's Catholic
    Church 75
St. Mary's Catholic
    Church 51, 96-97
St. Paul 240
Stafford County 31, 33
Stafford County Flour
    Mills 120-121
Stapleton #1 127
Steele Homestead 50
Sternberg Museum
    of Natural History 215
Stockton 124
Stoeber, Frank 44, 186
Stone Gallery 102
Suh, Do-Ho 99
Svaty, Josh: Commerce,
    introduction by 107
Swedish Country Inn 169
Swimming in the summer 187
Sylvan Grove 123

Tallgrass Prairie National
    Preserve 42-43
Tiffany Windows 104
Tipton 129

Topeka 50, 63, 76, 95, 103,
    104, 135, 150, 173, 180,
    231, 234, 260, 262
Topeka Civic Theatre 180
Topeka High School 76
Toronto 210
Traditions Soda &
    Sandwich 172
Tragic Prelude 94-95
Trail Days Cafe and Museum 223
Trail of Fame 221
Trapper's Bar and Grill 157

U.S. Cavalry Museum 229
Ulrich Museum of Art 102
Ulysses 73, 219
University of Kansas 71, 149,
    163, 255
Using post rock for fencing
    178-179

Victoria 41
Vincent 61
Vonada Stone Company
    122-123

Wabaunsee County 214
Wakeeney 173
Walker 61
Walking to school 187
Wallace County 213
Walnut Valley Festival 161
Wamego 165, 266
Wamego Historical
    Museum 266
Warkentin, Bernhard 261
Warkentin House
    Museum 261
Washington 117
Waverly 266
Welda 182
Wellsville 100
Wellsville Historical
    Museum 100
Wellsville Library 100
West Mineral 45, 109
Westmoreland 55, 173
Wetlands and Wildlife
    National Scenic Byway 31
Wetmore 183
WheatFields Bakery
    Cafe 148-149
Wheatland Cafe 121

White, William Allen 258-259;
    home 258-259
White Cloud 195
White Memorial Park 259
Wichita 45, 73, 77, 83, 102,
    105, 130, 155, 173, 262,
    265, 266
Wichita Art Museum 105
Wichita Aviation Industry 130
Wichita Carthalite 77
Wichita High School North:
    exterior paintings 105
Wichita-Sedgwick County
    Historical Museum 262, 266
Williamsburg 145
Windsor Hotel 77
Winfield 161
Winter Livestock 131
Wizard of Oz, The 165
Wolf Creek Environmental
    Education area 131
Wolf Creek Generating
    Station 131
World's Largest Souvenir
    Travel Plate 91

Zinc mining 238